OUN'

D0524156

A Student's Guide
To Molière

by

BRIAN MASTERS

HEINEMANN EDUCATIONAL BOOKS

0435 375 709 0 152 70

Heinemann Educational Books Ltd
Halley Court, Jordan Hill, Oxford OX2 8EJ
OXFORD   LONDON   EDINBURGH
MELBOURNE   SYDNEY   AUCKLAND
IBADAN   NAIROBI   GABORONE   HARARE
KINGSTON   PORTSMOUTH NH (USA)
SINGAPORE   MADRID

ISBN 0 435 37570 9

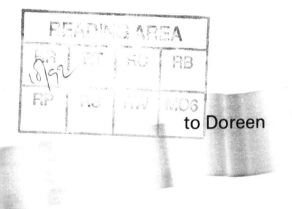

to Doreen

Printed and bound in Great Britain by
Biddles Ltd, Guildford and King's Lynn

Contents

Foreword

Acknowledgements

Foreword

This book is intended for the use of senior pupils in schools and students in colleges and universities. It attempts to summarize, as concisely as possible, the most important aspects of each of Molière's major plays, and also the most important critical appreciations, for which the student normally has to consult half a dozen different books.

What follows can in no way be considered a substitute for the personal reading of Molière's plays. Indeed, the student who turns to these pages before reading Molière would make precious little sense out of them, since any synopsis or summary of the plays is strictly avoided. It is hoped that the present marshalling of facts, characters, and critical impressions will be of help to the student after he has read the plays and will enable him to discern more clearly the bare bones of Molière's intention.

Furthermore, a handbook of this nature could not pretend to be exhaustive; it is meant as a brief introduction to more specialized studies. A select bibliography is to be found at the end of the book.

B.M.

The author wishes to thank Les Éditions Mondiales for permission to quote from *Histoire de la Littérature Française au XVIIe Siècle* by Antoine Adam, and the Librairie A. Hatier for their permission to quote from *Molière* by René Jasinski and *Molière* by Daniel Mornet. Special thanks are due to Madame René Bray, who has kindly allowed a passage to be included from her late husband's book *La Préciosité et les Précieux.*

1

Introduction

Jean-Baptiste Poquelin was born in a house on the rue Saint-Honoré in Paris on 15 January 1622, and baptized the same day. His father, Jean Poquelin, was an upholsterer by trade, and his mother, Marie Cressé, also came from a family of upholsterers. His uncle Nicholas was Official Upholsterer to the King, a position which he later ceded to his brother. The family, therefore, was solidly bourgeois and respectable, and showed no leanings or pretensions towards literary or theatrical talent. The young Jean-Baptiste was destined to become yet another upholsterer.

Our knowledge of Jean-Baptiste Poquelin's youth is severely limited, although quite a few million words must have been written around a network of inspired guesses and inventions. None of his works contain any hints about his early life, and he left no autobiography. No letter of his has survived. His friends and associates have not satisfied our curiosity with confidences. We are thus reduced to a handful of facts and probabilities, most of which are gleaned from the book published in 1682 by La Grange and Vinot, who were his contemporaries, supported by some very recent research.

His mother died when he was only ten years old. His father married again shortly afterwards, only to lose his second wife three years later. Five other children were born, of whom two died in infancy. Jean Poquelin sent his son to the Collège de Clermont, which is now the Lycée Louis le Grand, where we may assume he received a very good education. There is some evidence that he formed a plan to translate Lucretius at this time, which would show remarkable intelligence for a boy in his late teens, and would offer a clue as to the direction which his own thought would later take. It is at the school, according to legend, that he first made the acquaintance of the Prince de Conty, who later became a friend and patron, but Antoine Adam points out that this is unlikely, since the Prince was five years younger than Jean-Baptiste, and would therefore be just arriving at the school when the latter was leaving. It is more probable that he became friendly with Chapelle, whose family lodged the famous philosopher Gassendi in their house. According to tradition, Gassendi used to give private tuition to Chapelle and some of his school-friends, among whom was Jean-Baptiste Poquelin. If this is true, then it has a very important bearing on the work of Molière, Gassendi being the most notorious free thinker of his day. However, we must admit that this is something we cannot know for certain.

On leaving the Collège de Clermont, Jean-Baptiste studied law at Orléans, and was duly received at the bar, but he appears to have been an unsuccessful lawyer, for he lasted only a few months in the profession. Another tradition has it that the young man accompanied King Louis XIII on his journey to Narbonne in 1642, in place of his father.

This very shadowy outline only begins to take on a little substance when Jean-Baptiste reaches the age of twenty-one in 1643. At about this time he met the Béjart family, who were to be *his* family until his death. The eldest daughter Madeleine, twenty-four years old, was a beautiful girl of loose morals who had begun to make a name for herself as an actress. She represents Jean-Baptiste's first connection with the theatrical world, and probably his first love affair. He moved in to live with the family in the rue de Thorigny, and must then have decided to give up the Bar, and also renounce his succession to his father's hereditary position as Royal Upholsterer. He wanted to be an actor.

It must be remembered that there were more honourable professions than that of actor in seventeenth-century France. The theatre was commonly held to be a den of vice and sin, in which no decent Catholic citizen would become involved. Performances at the theatre frequently degenerated into ribald riots, and it was quite common for the audience to sit on the stage and heckle the actors. The life an actor led was supposed to be immoral, decadent, and anti-Christian. The Church was quite explicit in its condemnation; it spoke of 'publicly unworthy persons, such as people who have been excommunicated, and manifestly sordid persons, such as prostitutes, concubines, actors, usurers and witches.' Actors habitually ran the risk of automatic and arbitrary excommunication. When Molière died, two priests refused to come and administer the last rites, on the grounds that he was 'of the theatre' and therefore not entitled to a Christian death. On the other hand, it is true that many people who embraced the theatrical profession made a decent living out of it, and were courted by the nobility, though not always for noble reasons, and also that Louis XIV was a great patron of the arts, and encouraged the theatre with generous financial aid as well as moral support. However, the row over the morality of the theatre lasted well into the next century, with Rousseau's famous *Lettre à d'Alembert*, and might almost be said to continue in muted tones even now.

On 30 June 1643, the Illustre Théâtre was founded, led by Madeleine Béjart, Jean-Baptiste Poquelin, and six other actors. Soon afterwards, Poquelin changed his name to Molière (the signature first appears on a contract dated 28 June 1644), but we have no idea why he chose this particular stage name. The Illustre Théâtre company was ill-fated, played to near-empty houses, and folded after two years with a pile of unpaid bills. One François Pommier, a money-lender, had Molière (by this time the leader of the Company) sent to prison for a few days for not paying his debts.

After this fiasco had left them in material and spiritual ruins, they were forced either to join another company or to give up the theatre altogether. The Duke of Épernon, who thought highly of Madeleine Béjart's talents, came to the rescue. He was patron of a company led by Charles Dufresne, and he arranged for the three Béjarts and Molière to join his Company, which they did at the beginning of 1646.

For the next twelve years, Molière and his friends toured the provinces in the South of France, gaining valuable experience and sharpening their talents. They played in Carcassone, Nantes, Toulouse, Narbonne, Lyon, Pézenas, Grenoble, Montpellier, Avignon, returning several times to Pézenas with repeated success. Sometime before 1652, the Duke of Épernon withdrew his patronage from the group, and Dufresne ceded the Direction of the Company to Molière. In 1652, they found a new patron in the Prince de Conty, whose castle was near Pézenas, and who favoured the charms of one of the actresses, Mlle du Parc. This patronage was to last five years, until the Prince, converted to a sudden bigotry which accorded ill with allowing a group of actors to bear his name, withdrew his support in 1657, and became an implacable enemy.

Soon afterwards, Molière's players turned their gaze towards Paris. They were playing in Rouen in 1658, and arrived in Paris towards the end of that year. By this time, Molière was a different man from the young adventurer who left Paris in 1646. Larroumet exaggerates perhaps when he writes that 'Les Béjart emmènent avec Molière un déclassé, un fugitif de la maison paternelle [Molière remained on good terms with his father, who never objected to his joining the theatre], qui a tâté du Chatelet [the prison] et, dans douze ans, ils le ramèneront formé par l'expérience, riche d'impressions et de souvenirs, maître de lui-même et de son génie, mûr pour les chefs-d'oeuvre.' One must, however, admit that Molière now had a reputation, that his company was recognized to be one of the finest in France, and that it had grown to include another Béjart – Louis, two fine actresses in du Parc and de Brie, who were later to create some of his best parts. They were ready for the challenge of Paris.

The first performance which Molière and his Company gave in Paris took place in the Louvre Palace, before the King and his court, on 24 October 1658. The play was *Nicomède* which, by all accounts, was poorly received.

However, the evening was rounded off with a performance of *Le Docteur Amoureux*, one of the many short whimsical farces which the Company had presented with such success in the provinces. This piece of nonsense 'brought the house down' and resulted in the actors gaining a new patron in Monsieur Frère du Roi (the eighteen-year-old Duke of Orleans), and in the King offering them a theatre to play in, the Petit Bourbon, which they would have to share with the Italian Company, whose leader was Scaramouche. This in turn led to a lasting friendship between Molière and Scaramouche, which may well have contributed yet another influence on some of the comedies he was to write, and suggested to him many of the characters and plots which were the stock-in-trade of Scaramouche and the *Commedia dell'Arte*.

During the following winter, Molière's company underwent some important changes. First, death robbed them of one of their principal actors, Joseph Béjart, and retirement of another, Charles Dufresne, who had been the leader of the group when Molière and the Béjart family joined it. On the other hand, they made worthwhile recruits in Jodelet, a comic actor with an already fine reputation, Du Croisy, and Charles Varlet de la Grange.

The young La Grange was to prove an acquisition for which scholars have for ever been thankful. Only twenty years old when he joined Molière, he was to become both his most faithful friend and his successor. From the very beginning of their association, La Grange kept a record of the Company's fortunes, not a personal diary, but a detailed register, in which he noted all the performances and the circumstances surrounding many of them, right up to the death of Molière.

It is an invaluable document, the only contemporary testimony we have that is dispassionate and factual. La Grange was also to publish, together with Vinot, the first *Complete Works of Molière*, with an important Preface, in 1682. Finally La Grange it was who assumed the Directorship of the Company upon Molière's death in 1673.

Two of the productions which Molière presented in Paris during this first season were plays that he had written himself, *L'Étourdi* and *Le Dépit Amoureux*. The first was probably written in 1655, and the second almost certainly in 1656. They are the earliest known plays which were incontestably written by Molière himself, and as such represent the transition from actor to actor-playwright, and the first hesitant attempts of a genius. Jasinski goes so far as to claim that they provide the key to the whole of Molière's work. Neither play is original (few of Molière's plays ever invented an original plot). *L'Étourdi* copies the absurd intrigue of *L'Innavertito* of Barbieri (1629). *Le Dépit Amoureux* is taken from *L'Interesse* of Secchi (1581). They are Italian in inspiration and form, allowing the hand of Molière to show through only in a certain style of characterization.

It was not until the autumn of 1659, with *Les Précieuses Ridicules*, that the originality and audacity of Molière were first seen.

2

Les Précieuses Ridicules

Before we examine the principal ideas of Molière in this play, it is as well that we should have a clear understanding of what La Préciosité is. We cannot appreciate the joke before we appreciate its object.

La Préciosité was at once a literary and a social movement, essentially feminist, which had existed as a vague and voiceless attitude for several years, but which did not achieve the dignity of an articulate sect or côterie until the middle of the seventeenth century. Antoine Adam claims to have fixed the date quite definitely at 1654, when the Chevalier de Sévigné mentioned in a letter the existence of 'une nature de filles et de femmes à Paris que l'on nomme Précieuses, qui ont un jargon et des mines, avec un démanchement merveilleux'. A group of very earnest, crusading writers and literati, they met in salons to read each other's poetry and novels, to discuss literature in general, and to promote their own 'revolutionary' ideas. The most famous pure Précieux writers of the period are Mlle de Scudéry, Somaize, Voiture, l'abbé de Pure, l'abbé Cotin, and Honoré d'Urfé, but there are elements of the Précieux style and subject matter of the Précieuses in the works of Corneille, Boileau, Racine, and even Molière.

They had a very determined style of behaviour and speech as well as of writing. In their efforts to achieve purity of language, their everyday conversation was larded with heavy and laboured constructions and figures of speech, and often appeared to prefer the more difficult and long-winded expression to the more simple and concise. Nowadays, we would call them intellectual snobs. Somaize actually published a long list of maxims according to which the Précieuses were supposed to manage their lives and form their tastes, in his *Grand Diction-naire* (1661).

Préciosité consists essentially in the following ideas:

1. The establishment of an intellectual aristocracy; the effort to purify the French language, and champion its use as against the pre-eminence of the classical languages in literature.
2. The emancipation of women, especially in affairs of the heart, and the idea that love should be a pure, intellectual passion, rather than a carnal and sensual desire.

1. Intellectual aristocracy

(*a*) Somaize, in the work already referred to, claims that 'une pensée ne vaut rien lorsqu'elle est entendue de tout le monde'. Literature, if it is to be worth anything therefore, must not be readily understood and appreciated by the masses, but should be reserved for the select few, the intellectual élite.

(*b*) L'abbé de Pure encourages the writer to sustain a great effort of will in order that he should 'se tirer du prix commun des autres'.

(*c*) For l'abbé de Pure, the Précieuses are above all 'modernists'. They stand for the dignity of the French language, and react against the tradition that only the classical languages of Greek and Latin are worthy of a great work of art. (The great tragedies of Corneille, and later of Racine, were taken from classical tragedies, and the comedies of Rotrou were likewise adapted from classical precursors. The Précieuses were among the first in the seventeenth century to publish works whose inspiration was entirely French.)

(*d*) 'Il considère le style non comme un moyen, mais comme un

but. Autrement dit, c'est une forme particulière de l'art
pour l'art. . . .
. . . Mais, si les Précieux ne se trompent point en estimant
qu'il existe un art littéraire, où leur erreur commence,
c'est à croire que la littérature n'est qu'un art . . . la
littérature vit d'idées'.   (Emile Faguet, 1927)

Faguet's dismissal of Préciosité is not entirely justified, since
the poetry of Voiture, for example, is not lacking in ideas.

2. The emancipation of women

(*a*) La Préciosité est essentiellement, non pas une attitude en
face de l'art et des lettres, mais une position prise devant
les problèmes de la vie sentimentale . . . Les Précieuses
sont d'abord des femmes qui se révoltent contre le joug
du mariage et contre la lourde discipline que les moeurs
coñtinuent d'imposer à la jeune fille. Elles affirment le
droit de la femme de disposer librement d'elle-même, à
choisir le compagnon de la vie, à cultiver, s'il lui plaît,
avant et durant le mariage, l'art et les belles lettres, à
connaître les plaisirs de l'esprit.
                    (Antoine Adam, 'Baroque et Préciosité',
                    in *La Revue des Sciences Humaines*, 1949)

(*b*) In early-seventeenth-century France, the girl was still very
much an inferior being, subject to her father's will and whim,
and liable to be married off by him to someone whom she
had never met, let alone loved. The Précieuses rebelled
against this custom, and in this at least, Molière clearly
agreed with them. They were, therefore, a kind of militant,
sentimental, feminist movement. Madeleine de Scudéry, in
her *Cyrus*, criticized men who:

'ne regardant les femmes que comme les premières esclaves
de leurs maisons, défendoient à leurs filles de lire jamais
d'autres livres que ceux qui leur servoient à prier les dieux,
et qui ne vouloient point qu'elles chantassent les chansons
de Sapho', and women who 'pensant que la vertu scrupuleuse vouloit qu'une femme ne sût rien faire autre chose
que d'être femme de son mari, mère de ses enfants et

maîtresse de sa famille et de ses esclaves, trouvoient que Sapho et ses amis donnoient trop de temps à la conversation'.

(c) In matters of the heart, women must show their independence and superiority over mere carnal pleasure by purifying and intellectualizing the concept of love. Love was to become a mystical union between two souls, not an expression of low desire. Hence Ninon de Lenclos called the Précieuses 'Les Jansénistes de l'amour', since the Jansenists of Port-Royal, named after the Dutch theologian Cornelius Jansen, sought a similar mystical union with God.

(d) Elles veulent l'amour, mais un amour qui soit essentiellement liberté . . . en face des passions sensuelles. Elles ne veulent aimer que par un pur choix de l'esprit . . . l'amour, chez elles, sera quelque chose de très intellectuel, de très conscient.   (Antoine Adam, ibid)

(e) In *Clélie*, Mlle de Scudéry published an allegorical map to show the route to ideal love which her heroine had taken, along a river called 'Inclination' which led from 'Nouvelle Amitié' to 'Tendre-sur-Estime', two towns marked on the map. Villages on the way bore such names as 'Grand Esprit', 'Jolis Vers', 'Billet-doux', being such stratagems as might help achieve the goal, but to get there quicker, one had necessarily to pass through 'Sincérité', 'Grand Coeur', 'Probité', 'Générosité', 'Respect', 'Exactitude' and 'Bonté', this latter being the most important, since 'il ne peut y avoir de véritable estime sans bonté et qu'on ne peut arriver à "Tendre" de ce côté-là sans avoir cette précieuse qualité'. This map was known as *La Carte du Tendre*, and carried almost biblical authority with the followers and admirers of Mlle de Scudéry. Molière makes reference to it in the text of his play.

The most accomplished modern expert on Préciosité is René Bray, whose book *La Préciosité et les Précieux* (1948), is the most important work of reference on the subject. From it, we take the following few sentences:

(i) Il est alogique . . . il n'aime pas les voies battues du raisonnement.

(ii) Il vise à la surprise . . . la nouveauté, l'inouïe, l'inédit. Il se nourrit d'originalité.

(iii) Plus un esprit est cultivé, plus il est susceptible à la Préciosité. L'art précieux naît avec la civilization.

(iv) Un art subjectif . . . une danse devant le miroir.

(v) Son seul Dieu, c'est la Beauté. Le seul critérium dont il se serve pour juger son oeuvre, c'est celui de la forme.

and lastly, a superb formula which catches perfectly the artistic dilletantism of the Précieuses: 'Le jeu inutile et sans cause d'un oisif à l'esprit agile et à l'imagination féconde'.

The Heritage of Préciosité

Although Antoine Adam carries much authority, it would be wrong to regard his 1654 as a magical date on which this social and literary style 'suddenly' burst upon the scene. Préciosité, in one form or another, had flourished many years before, and not only in France. In the thirteenth century, Guillaume de Lorris's famous *Roman de la Rose* sprang clearly from a similar inspiration to the vast, rambling Précieux novels of the mid-seventeenth century. There followed the works of Rotrou, Nervèze, Escuteaux, Théophile and others, in the early decades of the seventeenth century. A particular variant of Précieux poetry was written by the Italian Marini (1569–1625) and the Spaniard Gongora (1561–1627). In England, too, the novelist John Lyly was already anticipating the fashion in the sixteenth century. One might even say that Seneca indulged in a little extravagance of style and language, and many writers in our own day are tarred with the same brush. The element which unites these many disparate writers is a concern to make their language enchanting, their expression perfect, their choice of word exact. In 1659 in France, however, the fashion had reached a point where its more serious aspects had been submerged beneath an ocean of silly euphemisms, exaggerated metaphors, extraordinary allegories, unusual epigrams, absurd sentence constructions, and the mere fad of using a long word where a short one would have served better. The ideal of intellectual love, which was celebrated in pungent epigrams and which never entered between bedsheets, had been developed out of all proportion.

Principal Ideas and Themes of the Play

A. Molière's Preface
1. Les plus excellentes choses sont sujettes à être copiées par de mauvais singes, qui méritent d'être bernés; ces vicieuses imitations de ce qu'il y a de plus parfait ont été de tout temps la matière de la comédie.
2. Les véritables précieuses auraient tort de se piquer, lorsqu'on joue les ridicules qui les imitent mal.

B. Langage Précieux
1. Vite, voiturez-nous ici les commodités de la conversation. [i.e. approchez les chaises]   (Magdalon, Sc. IX)
2. Mais de grâce, Monsieur, ne soyez pas inexorable à ce fauteuil qui vous tend les bras il y a un quart d'heure; contentez un peu l'envie qu'il a de vous embrasser.
    (Cathos, Sc. IX)
3. Je vous avoue que je suis furieusement pour les portraits.
    (Magdalon, Sc. IX)

This last remark has come full circle since the seventeenth century, and now forms once again part of fashionable language, as in, for example, 'I'm terribly fond of music', or 'You're frightfully well read'.

C. Marriage
1. Le mariage est une chose sainte et sacrée, et c'est faire en honnêtes gens que de débuter par là.
    (Gorgibus, Sc. IV)

This bourgeois point of view contrasts with the flamboyant feminism of the précieuses:

2. c'est prendre le roman par la queue.
                                             (Magdalon, Sc. IV)
3. je trouve le mariage une chose tout à fait choquante.
                                             (Cathos, Sc. IV)

D. Le Bel Esprit de L'Époque
1. Mais je vous demande d'applaudir comme il faut . . . c'est
   la coutume ici qu'à nous autres gens de condition, les
   auteurs viennent lire leurs pièces nouvelles, pour nous
   engager à les trouver belles et leur donner de la réputation.
                                             (Mascarille, Sc. IX)
2. Les gens de qualité savent tout sans avoir jamais rien
   appris.   (Mascarille, Sc. IX)
3. Il n'y a rien à meilleur marché que le bel esprit de main-
   tenant.   (La Grange, Sc. I)

E. The Language of Gorgibus: contrast with Précieux language
1. Il est bien nécessaire, vraiment, de faire tant de dépense
   pour vous graisser le museau.

It is unlikely that Molière prefers this vulgar and crude language; but it is amusing, and it serves to emphasize the absurdity
of the Précieuses. This character is not supposed to embody an
ideal, but to place in perspective, by his false wisdom, the ridiculous performance of his daughter and of his niece.

F. A faithful picture?
By no means. Molière distorts the truth. He admits this in his
own preface, and we have already seen what were the ideals of
the true Précieuses. He is writing a comedy, and presents an
hilarious caricature, not a faithful portrait.

His play is in form a farce – but it is also a satire of a personal
nature. Says Antoine Adam, 'Molière est le premier qui ait
consacré une pièce de théâtre à faire la satire d'une mode, et
pis encore, une satire personnelle, qui atteignait des personnages
connus'. However, others had attacked the abuse of Préciosité
before him, notably Scarron and Saint-Evremond.

One must also bear in mind that Molière agreed with the
Précieuses in many respects, especially with their idea that real

virtue did not require rigid discipline, and in fact was more likely to be suffocated by it. This is an idea which occurs throughout his work.

cf. *Maupertuis*: Le bel esprit n'est le plus souvent que l'art de donner à une pensée commune un tour sententieux.

cf. *La Bruyère*: il fallait de l'esprit, non pas du meilleur, mais de celui qui est faux, et où l'imagination a trop de part.   (Les Caractères, V)

The encouraging success of *Les Précieuses Ridicules* was followed by another one-act farce, *Sganarelle ou Le Cocu Imaginaire*, in May 1660, which is interesting if only because Sganarelle is the prototype of a character who is later to recur in many of the plays and to achieve his greatest incarnation as Arnolphe in *L'École des Femmes*.

On 4 February 1661 Molière presented *Dom Garcie de Navarre*, a much less popular type of entertainment, which flopped badly. Scholars have lingered over it because they have seen in it the germs of *Le Misanthrope*, and indeed have identified some of the speeches of the latter masterpiece in this sadly boring play.

The three-act *École des Maris*, first seen on 24 June 1661, successfully uses for the first time the formula which forms the backbone for some of the later comedies – the struggle between youth and ignorant old age. The central character, Sganarelle, is a stupid little man with a false idea of his importance and intelligence, easy prey to flattery, who is easily outwitted by his daughter and her lover, Isabelle and Valère, youthful, charming, endowed with natural intelligence and guile. There is another character, Ariste, Sganarelle's brother, who will also turn up under many other names. This is the first appearance of the 'raisonneur', a stock Molière character whom some critics have seen as the level-headed, confident, sensible adviser amid the confusion of interests and emotions. We shall consider him in his place.

3
L'École des Femmes

Molière's first five-act play received its first performance on 26 December 1662, and was dedicated to Henriette d'Angleterre.[1] With *L'École des Femmes*, Molière assured his place as one of the finest and most controversial writers in the theatre. The play set in motion a great wave of invective and scandal-mongering which sought to vilify not merely Molière's art, but also his private life; it was variously condemned as irreligious, immoral and obscene. At the same time, it was recognized to be extremely funny.

Arnolphe is a middle-aged bachelor who wants an ideal wife – faithful, obedient, servile and ignorant. In order to achieve this object, he has brought up from childhood a beautiful young girl, Agnès, whom he intends to marry when she is properly trained. He has kept her entirely removed from the world, forbidden her to read books, or to meet people, and hopes that now, as she flowers into womanhood, she is ready to marry him, whether she likes it or not, and make him the perfect, unquestioning wife. But Agnès falls in love with a handsome young man, Horace, whose ingenuity and intelligence succeed in pulling the wool over the old man's eyes, while at the same time providing fuel for his jealousy. The young lovers are finally united by a most improbable dénouement, which calls for Agnès's father suddenly to appear from America to reveal that he gives his daughter in marriage to Horace, the son of his best friend!

[1] First wife of Monsieur, the king's brother, who was still at this time Molière's patron.

A. Arnolphe

1. Arnolphe est un fantoche, petit de taille, sautillant, ironique et pointu, ahuri et berné comme Sganarelle.

(Antoine Adam)

Arnolphe is in fact much the same character as Sganarelle, who precedes him in 1660, (in *L'École des Maris*), and Harpagon, who follows him in 1668 (in *L'Avare*). He is stubborn and self-opinionated, with ready-made ideas which will admit no compromise and lead him to believe passionately that everybody else is wrong and only he is right. Consequently, he is blind to what is happening under his very nose, and he will not be enlightened. He spurns all advice, since he is convinced that he is the wisest man in the world. He has scant respect for the notion of conjugal equality. Furthermore, and this is how Molière achieves the pathos of the character, he is basically afraid of women.

When, in Scene IV of Act 5, he sees finally that youth and innocence have triumphed over all his cunning, he becomes at once a ridiculous and pathetic figure, trying grotesquely to declare love to Agnès. Nothing will prevent him from following his 'idée fixe'. He speaks himself of his 'sick mind' and recognizes his stubbornness:

2. En femme, comme en tout, je veux suivre ma mode.

(Act 1, Sc. I)

3. . . . les soupçons de *mon esprit malade*.

(Act 2, Sc. IV) (our italics)

When Arnolphe becomes righteous, angry or indignant, the servants, Alain and Georgette, are not in the slightest afraid of him; they only pretend to be, while in fact they are making fun of him. He, who wants more than anything the respect which his age demands, has made himself the laughing stock of his household.

B. Agnès

1. Molière décrit avec tendresse cette naissance d'une âme à

la vie. Il la décrit lucide et consciente de tout ce qui lui manque encore, courageuse et qui brave son tyran. Quand Arnolphe veut la persuader qu'elle commet le mal [in Act 5, Scene IV], cette enfant a des mots qui réduisent les sophismes du pédant. Elle est la simple, la pure raison en face des routines imbéciles. (Antoine Adam)

Agnès is charmingly frank and open in her language, since her severe upbringing has kept her ignorant of the niceties of polite conversation. At her entrance (Act 1, Sc. III), she admits that the fleas have troubled her during the night, and thus, in one line, establishes her sheltered innocence.

But this innocence, carefully nurtured by Arnolphe, cannot stifle the natural intelligence and guile of her youth. In all her simplicity, she is much wiser than Arnolphe, and can be brutally, cruelly, devastatingly honest and forthright:

2. Chez vous le mariage est fâcheux et pénible. Et vos discours en font une image terrible. (Act 5, Sc. IV)

3. Tenez, tous vos discours ne me touchent point l'âme. Horace avec deux mots en ferait plus que vous. (Act 5, Sc. IV)

Above all, Agnès possesses the rare virtue of ingenuousness, the result of her being kept in ignorance. She has an unspoilt, generous, sensitive nature, which the fanatical threats of Arnolphe cannot stifle. 'Tout en elle est sourire', says Jasinski.

C. Chrysalde

1. Il faut, comme en tout, fuir les extrémités. (Act 4, Sc. VIII)

2. Si n'être point cocu vous semble un si grand bien. Ne vous point marier en est le vrai moyen. (Act 5, Sc. IX)

These two quotations perfectly summarize the character of Chrysalde, particularly his facile cautiousness. It would, however, be a serious mistake to consider, as some critics have done, that Chrysalde represents the measured view of Molière himself. He is no more Molière's spokesman than was the first 'raisonneur', Ariste in *L'École des Maris*. Indeed, Molière's philosophy would be thin if it rested on such superficial moralizing as this. We shall have more to say about the 'juste milieu' fallacy in the final chapter, but for the moment, we shall leave the last word again with Antoine Adam:

> 3. Ce prétendu sage enseigne aux maris, non pas du tout la sagesse, mais une complaisance ridicule. Il le fait avec une platitude d'expression et une bassesse de pensée qu'il ne faut pas prendre au sérieux. Le bon sens prend dans la bouche du raisonneur une allure bouffonne, et lorsqu'il développe pesamment qu'au fait de cocuage il faut fuir toute extrémité, comprenons bien que Molière alors veut nous faire rire de cette drôlerie, et non point du tout révéler sa morale.

D. Alain et Georgette

The two peasants are crude in language and sly in money matters. Their scenes introduce the only element of farce in the play, provoking a hearty laugh rather than the more subtle smile of reflection which most of the other scenes excite.

> 1. Ah, vous me faites peur, et tout mon sang se fige.
> (Georgette, Act 2, Sc. II)
> 2. La femme est en effet le potage de l'homme,
> Et, quand un homme voit d'autres hommes parfois
> Qui veulent dans sa soupe aller tremper leurs doigts,
> Il en montre aussitôt une colère extrême.
> (Alain, Act 2, Sc. III)

We should notice, incidentally, the consummate skill with which Molière puts the poor language of the uneducated peasant into verse, as well as the vulgarity of the image itself; this is one of the scenes which shocked so many of the contemporaries, and went some way to cause the scandal which ensued.

E. Principal Ideas of the Play

1. On love, and its power to enlighten

    (*a*) Il le faut avouer, l'amour est un grand maître.
        Ce qu'on ne fut jamais, il nous enseigne à l'être.
                        (Horace, Act 3, Sc. IV)
    (*b*) L'amour sait-il pas l'art d'aiguiser les esprits? (idem)

2. On the education of girls

    (*a*) Mais une femme habile est un mauvais présage.
                       (Arnolphe, Act I, Sc. I)
    (*b*) Et c'est assez pour elle, à vous en bien parler,
        De savoir prier Dieu, m'aimer, coudre et filer.' (idem)

This is the false view, which Molière wishes to satirize, and
which he does with increasing vehemence throughout his plays;
it is significant that the first requirement, in Arnolphe's mind,
is that his wife should 'savoir prier Dieu'.

In his attempts to secure his wife's obedience, Arnolphe invokes
the fires of Hell. Can there be any question that he is a religious
fanatic, and that Molière wishes to make a statement on the
evil power of religion?

3. On marriage

Again, the narrow-minded, harsh, sometimes absurd view which
Molière despises:

    (*a*) Votre sexe n'est là que pour la dépendance:
        Du côté de la barbe est la toute-puissance.
                      (Arnolphe, Act 3, Sc. II)

    (*b*) . . . du profond respect, que la femme doit être
        Pour son mari, son chef, son seigneur et son maître.
                              (idem)

    (*c*) . . . il est aux enfers des chaudières bouillantes
        Où l'on plonge à jamais les femmes mal vivantes. (idem)

    (*d*) Entre les austères et ceux de la cour et des belles
        compagnies, *L'École des Maris* et *L'École des Femmes*

prennent simplement le parti de la cour et des belles
compagnies.   (Daniel Mornet)

4. The Moral and the Argument

For Daniel Mornet, there is a conflict in the play between two
aspects of Christian morality, (a) that a daughter must obey
her father at all times and in all things, (b) that God has given
us passions and desires which we can at will use for good or
evil purposes, but which are not to be denied, but encouraged
to healthy expression. Therefore, it is wrong to see the play as
blasphemous or immoral.

Antoine Adam, on the other hand, sees the underlying moral
quite differently. He reproaches certain critics for refusing to
recognize in *L'École des Femmes* a satire on Christian morality.
He asks whether it is possible to find in any other play of the
period one scene in which the idea of sin is questioned with
such frankness as it is by Agnès:

> Molière a pour toute morale ascétique une hostilité
> raisonnée et de principe, . . . il fait confiance à la vie, à la
> spontanéité, à la liberté. Non pas qu'il aboutisse à l'exalta-
> tion de l'instinct, ou de la Nature. Mais l'effort de culture
> morale où il met son idéal lui semble incompatible avec la
> contrainte extérieure.
> Son audace est de porter sur la scène, de couvrir de ridicule
> les défenseurs de la morale traditionelle, les tenants de
> l'ascétisme.   (Antoine Adam)

4

La critique de L'École des Femmes

First of all, a brief résumé of the principal stages in the polemic which followed *L'École des Femmes*:

I January 1663: Si tu savais un peu moins plaire
                 Tu ne leur déplairais pas tant.' (Boileau)
February 1663: *Nouvelles Nouvelles*, by Donneau de Visé
I June 1663: *Critique de L'École des Femmes*, by Molière
September 1663: *Le Portrait du Peintre*, by Boursault
4 November 1663: *L'Impromptu de Versailles*, by Molière.

The storm broke after the very first performance of Molière's play, with far more writers rushing into print to attack the author than to defend him. Boileau was very much in a minority when he wrote his famous couplet quoted above, and at the time he was an unknown young poet to whom nobody paid very much attention. For the most part, it was left to Molière to defend himself, though he did write *L'Impromptu de Versailles* at the express request of the King. He also appears to have needed no small courage to stand up to his adversaries, so strong was the feeling against him. According to one story, Molière received an anonymous letter threatening that he would be 'beaten up' ('des coups de bâtons') if he dared to put on *La Critique de L'École des Femmes*.

A. The Charges

1. That the play was obscene, spattered with coarse jokes, vulgar inferences and indecencies, such as the references to 'tarte à la crème' and 'enfants par l'oreille', a wife being a

man's soup into which other men should not dip their fingers, and the shocking ambiguity of the word 'le' in Scene V of Act 2. It was a play which 'tient la pudeur en alarme' and 'salit l'imagination'. The Prince de Conty (Molière's erstwhile patron) wrote that 'il n'y a rien de plus scandaleux que la cinquième scène du deuxième acte de *L'École des Femmes*.'

2. That Arnolphe's maxims for marriage were a blasphemous parody of the ten commandments, and that religion was thereby ridiculed.

3. That the play was not written according to the famous classical 'rules' of the theatre, i.e. unity of time, place, and character. Also, of course, by virtue of point (1) above, the play sinned against the classical credo of the 'bienséances'.

4. A personal affront which was voiced later, according to which the relationship between Arnolphe and Agnès formed a parallel with Molière's own relationship with his wife Armande. Molière had married Armande Béjart on 20 February 1662, less than a year before the play was produced. She was said to be the younger sister of Madeleine Béjart, but there was a suspicion that she might in fact be Madeleine's daughter, and since Molière had known Madeleine for nearly twenty years, his enemies later went so far as to suggest that he was Armande's own father, and that their marriage was incestuous. It must be said that there is absolutely no evidence to support this accusation, though speculation has persisted on the matter until the present day.[1] In any case, it has nothing whatever to do with the play, and it is the one charge to which Molière never replied. (It is nevertheless true that Armande was not a faithful wife, and her incorrigible flirting may well have suggested the character of Célimène in *Le Misanthrope*.)

---

[1] The student who wishes to pursue further the matter of Armande Béjart's identity should read *l'Etat Civil d'Armande Béjart* by Georges Couton, in *la Revue des Sciences Humaines*, July to September 1964.

B. Molière's Reply

In *La Critique*, Molière takes the opportunity (1) to set forth some of his own ideas on the art of comedy and the relevance of 'les règles', (2) to answer his critics on specific points, (3) to further satirize some social types, many of which were based on actual contemporaries. According to Boursault, an index was published revealing the names of the people whom Molière was satirizing, but if this is true, the index has now been lost, and we can only guess their identity.

1. The aims of Comedy

> de rendre agréablement sur le théâtre les défauts de tout le monde. Vous n'avez rien fait, si vous n'y faites reconnaître les gens de votre siècle. (Dorante, Sc. VI)

2. Les Règles

> (*a*) La grande règle de toutes les règles est de plaire.
> (Dorante, Sc. VI)

> (*b*) si les pièces qui sont selon les règles ne plaisent pas et celles qui plaisent ne soient pas selon les règles, il faudrait de nécessité que les règles eussent été mal faites.
> (ibid)

3. Complexity of Character

In life, people are rarely completely coherent in their personality or their actions, and since the theatre is taken from life, theatrical characters would be artificial if they were predictable.

> il n'est pas incompatible qu'une personne soit ridicule en de certaines choses et honnête homme en d'autres.
> (Dorante, Sc. VI)

4. Comedy of Manners

> ces sortes de satires tombent directement sur les moeurs, et ne frappent les personnes que par réflexion.
> (Uranie, Scene VI)

5. *The good judgement of the gallery*

le bon sens n'a point de place déterminée à la comédie; la différence du demi-louis d'or et la pièce de 15 sous ne fait rien du tout au bon goût.   (Dorante, Sc. V)

6. *Defence of the Court*

la grande épreuve de toutes vos comédies, c'est le jugement de la Cour; c'est son goût qu'il faut étudier pour trouver l'art de réussir . . . simple bon sens naturel.
                                            (Dorante, Sc. VI)

C. Molière Ridicules . . .

1. *Les Précieuses*

il semble que tout son corps soit démonté, et que les mouvements de ses hanches, de ses épaules et de sa tête n'aillent que par ressorts. Elle affecte toujours un ton de voix languissant et niais . . . roule les yeux pour les faire paraître grands.   (Élise, Sc. II)

2. *Les Prudes*

(*a*) L'honnêteté d'une femme n'est pas dans les grimaces.
                                            (Uranie, Sc. III)

(*b*) il y a des personnes qui se rendent ridicules pour vouloir avoir trop d'honneur . . . celles qui, étant sur le retour de l'âge, veulent remplacer de quelque chose ce qu'elles voient qu'elles perdent, et prétendent que les grimaces d'une pruderie scrupuleuse leur tiendront lieu de jeunesse et de beauté.   (Dorante, Sc. V)

3. *The self-appointed marquesses*

(*a*) ces gens qui parlent hardiment de toutes choses, sans s'y connaître.   (Dorante, Sc. V)

(*b*) Une douzaine de Messieurs qui déshonorent les gens de cour par leurs manières extravagantes et font croire parmi le peuple que nous nous ressemblons tous.
                                            (Dorante, Sc. V)

The fraudulent, self-appointed marquess was a common object of derision at this period. Madame de Sévigné wrote in 1675,

> Quand un homme veut usurper un titre, c'est celui de marquis, qui est tellement gâté, qu'en vérité je pardonne à ceux qui l'ont abandonné.

L'Impromptu de Versailles hit hard at the actors of the Hotel de Bourgogne. Molière parodied their extravagant language and gestures, and provoked a reply from the actor Montfleury a month later. The marquesses also come in for another attack, and Molière takes pains to show, in a long passage which reminds one of La Bruyère and of Molière's own creation, Alceste, that he has by no means exhausted all the stupidities and inanities of mankind which are fair game for the writer of comedy. He defends the comedy of Manners, which is not a personal attack on anyone.

Molière's personal relation with the Royal Family continued to be happy. In January 1664, the King and Queen agreed to be godparents to his first son, Louis. One can well imagine the fury of Molière's enemies.

5

Tartuffe

With cries of indecency and impropriety still ringing in his ears, it was almost logical that Molière should next turn his scorn on the moral and religious hypocrisy which lay behind them. Apart from the writing of a brief comedy-ballet, *Le Mariage Forcé*, performed on 29 January 1664, the months following the Quarrel of *L'École des Femmes* were spent preparing a work which was to bring down upon Molière attacks and defamations of even greater bitterness and intensity. This work was *Tartuffe*.

In May 1664 there took place at Versailles a sort of cultural festival called the Plaisirs de l'Île Enchantée. On 8 May, Molière presented to the Court a harmless little piece called *La Princesse d'Élide*, then followed it on the 12th with the first three acts of his so far unfinished play, *Tartuffe*. The reaction was immediately hostile, and the King was subjected to pressures from the Archbishop of Paris and from the Queen Mother to ban the play. On 17 May, an announcement appeared in the *Gazette* forbidding any public performance of *Tartuffe*. Thus began a polemic which was to continue for five years and was effectively to prevent Molière from giving any public showing of his play during this time. One writer called him 'un démon vêtu de chair et habillé en homme, et le plus signalé impie et libertin qui fut jamais'. He fought back by writing a pamphlet to the King in defence of the play (*Premier Placet*), then by attempting to present it under the title of *L'Imposteur* in 1667. (According to La Grange, the last two acts were completed by November 1664, which seems to indicate that the attacks, far

from silencing Molière, had encouraged him to finish the play.)
The day after the first performance of *L'Imposteur*, it was banned by the First President of the Parliament of Paris, Lamoignon. Molière protested to the King again, but was answered with a damning interdiction from the Archbishop who threatened anyone who produced, read, or attended a reading of Molière's play with immediate excommunication. ('... représenter, lire ou entendre réciter la susdite comédie, ... et ce, sous peine d'excommunication'). It was not until 9 February 1669 that the author felt free to attempt a third production of his play, this time under the original title and in five acts. By this time, the Queen Mother was dead. Between the first attempt in 1664 and the final success in 1669, Molière wrote seven other plays, including *Dom Juan, Le Misanthrope* and *L'Avare*.[1]

A. Les Caractères

1. Tartuffe

The primary motive for all his words and deeds is lust, thinly hidden beneath a fine turn of phrase, a 'gift of the gab', and a supremely insolent hypocrisy.

(*a*) Couvrez ce sein que je ne saurais voir.   (Act 3, Sc. II)

(*b*) Je n'ai pu vous, parfaite créture. Sans admirer en vous
l'auteur de la nature.   (Act 3, Sc. III)

(*c*) Ah! pour être dévot, je n'en suis pas moins homme.
                                                (Act 3, Sc. III)

(*d*) Et ce n'est pas pécher que pécher en silence. (Act 4, Sc. V)

Tartuffe insinuates himself into the household, makes himself the complete master of it in the guise of being a 'directeur de conscience', preaches extreme asceticism 'sous le pompeux éclat d'un austère grimace', and convinces both Orgon and

---

[1] Molière had also been favoured, in the interim, by the King's personal patronage. From 14 August 1664, when the memory of the outcry against the first version of *Tartuffe* was still fresh, Molière's company became known as the Troupe du Roi un Palais-Royal.

Madame Pernelle of his sincerity. He strikes his chest, lifts his eyes towards Heaven, accuses himself of all sins imaginable – 'Chaque instant de ma vie est chargé de souillures.'

The weakness which gives him away is his love, or passion, for Elmire. Every time he sees her, he loses his head, forgets his usual control, tries clumsily to speak in mystical and lyrical terms. This is what makes him funny. In the two seduction scenes, he expresses the most lustful thoughts in the most lyrical language. When he thinks he has achieved his object, he drops all pretence and reveals his true, sensual, nature:

> (e) Leur miel dans tous mes sens fait couler à longs traits
>   Une suavité qu'on ne goûta jamais.   (Act 4, Sc. V)

This is how Adam sees him:

> Il est gros et frais, la bouche vermeille, gros appétit, grosse nature. Il n'a rien d'un raffiné, il n'a ni culture, ni l'esprit, ni manières délicates. Il a commencé par mendier dans les églises. Ce n'est pas un aventurier séduisant, ce n'est qu'un bas coquin.'

> Jasinski, on the other hand, sees Tartuffe as 'un aventurier sans entrailles', and considers that 'il met en pleine lumière ce que peut le cynisme sous le couvert de la religion'.

Orgon thinks he is a 'gentilhomme', but, as Dorine points out, only because Tartuffe himself has said he is, and 'cette vanité ne sied pas bien avec la piété'.

When he puts his hand on Elmire's knee, and fingers her dress, his actions are almost unconscious. He always loses his self-control when he is face to face with a desirable woman.

For Tartuffe, religion is a means to an end; he is ambitious, using the blind naïvety of Orgon as his tool. But the audience is allowed to see through him, to observe the contrast between what he says and what he would like to say, what he does and what he thinks, and it is this which makes him a comic character. Moreover, he is the most perfectly observed incarnation of the eternal hypocrite. Molière's insight into the hidden motives of human conduct rarely found more consummate expression. As Jasinski has written:

> 'avec Tartuffe se fixe en effet pour jamais la psychologie du faux dévot.'

2. Orgon

Orgon belongs to the same gallery as Sganarelle (*L'École des Maris*) and Arnolphe (*L'École des Femmes*). He is happy in the knowledge that he is right and everyone else is wrong. His greatest joy is to 'faire enrager le monde'. He is also extremely naïve, as Tartuffe himself says, 'un homme, entre nous, à mener par le nez'. He is fundamentally a good man, corrupted by the evil influence of Tartuffe. In the third scene of Act 4, he is about to melt before the tender pleas of his daughter, but he finally closes his heart to affection and sentimentality. His unquestioning respect for Tartuffe has grown into a ridiculous and immoral infatuation; immoral, because it stifles all natural paternal feelings within him. He even intends to marry his daughter off to Tartuffe against her wishes, and to deprive his son of his rightful inheritance. The stupidity of one member of a family threatening to destroy the happiness and unity of the whole family is a recurrent theme in Molière's plays:

(a) Il l'appelle son frère et l'aime dans son âme
Cent fois plus qu'il ne fait mère, fils, fille et femme.
(Cléante)

(b) Orgon et Argan (in *Le Malade Imaginaire*) sont une seule et même personne soumise à des hypnoses différentes. L'un est fasciné par le salut de son âme, l'autre par le salut de son corps.   (R. Fernandez)

3. Cléante

(a) Les hommes, la plupart, sont étrangement faits,
Dans la juste nature on ne les voit jamais.
(Act 1, Sc.V)

(b) Et la plus noble chose, ils la gâtent souvent
Pour la vouloir outrer et pousser trop avant.   (idem)
(c) Aucune chose au monde et plus noble et plus belle
Que la sainte ferveur d'un véritable zèle,
Aussi ne vois-je rien qui soit plus odieux
Que le dehors plâtré d'un zèle spécieux.   (idem)
(d) C'est être libertin que d'avoir de bons yeux.   (idem)
(e) Les discours de Cléante, dans lesquels les vertus vraies et
éclairées sont opposées à la dévotion imbécile d'Orgon
sont le plus fort et le plus élégant sermon que nous ayons
en notre langue.   (Voltaire)

The view that Cléante expresses Molière's own religious
opinions, and his plea for indulgence, generosity and tolerance
in matters of worship, is one which is upheld by modern critics
such as R. Jasinski.

4. Dorine, Elmire, Mme Pernelle

Like all Molière's servants, Dorine speaks with unbridled
frankness. Her peasant good sense and insolence lend her an
authority which makes Orgon's spluttering protestations
ridiculous. She calls a spade a spade, and speaks her mind at the
slightest provocation.

Elmire is the only real Christian in the play. She allows herself to be seduced by Tartuffe only to show the truth to her
husband and rescue him from his delusion.

Madame Pernelle is as dogmatic and stubborn as Orgon.
She also speaks frankly, 'je ne mâche point ce que j'ai sur le
coeur.'

B. Views On . . .

1. Prudes

(a) Hautement d'un chacun elles blâment la vie
Non point par charité, mais par un trait d'envie
Qui ne saurait souffrir qu'une autre ait les plaisirs
Dont le penchant de l'âge a sevré leurs désirs.
(Dorine, Act 1, Sc. I)
(b) Je veux une vertu qui ne soit point diablesse. (Elmire)

2. Marriage

> Sachez que d'une fille on risque la vertu
> Lorsque dans son hymen son goût est combattu.
> (Dorine)

C. Molière's Intentions

(*a*) Le devoir de la comédie étant de corriger les hommes en
les divertissant, j'ai cru que dans l'emploi où je me trouve,
je n'avais rien de mieux à faire que d'attaquer, par des
peintures ridicules, les vices de ce siècle.
(Molière, ler. placet)

(*b*) Si l'emploi de la comédie est de corriger les vices des
hommes, je ne vois pas par quelle raison il y en aura de
privilégiés.   (Molière, Preface to *Tartuffe*)

Some critics have attempted to reduce *Tartuffe* to a mere story
of cuckoldry, claiming that Molière is not a satirist or a re-
former, but simply an entertainer. It is true that Molière defended himself against attack with the plea that his intentions
were 'partout innocentes', but in the circumstances it is under-
standable that he should thus play down the satirical content
of his work. It is clear from the Preface, from both placets, and
from the text, that Molière wishes to denounce a bigotry which
he detests. (This does not mean to say, however, that he was
giving expression in this play to his own thinly-concealed
atheism, as some fanciful critics have claimed.)

What then is Molière's own conception of Christianity, as
seen in his play? Religion is a private and intensely personal
road to happiness and peace of mind, which should inspire
Love and Virtue. It is foreign to the idea of sects and militant
groups, and in particular runs counter to one essential maxim
of religious orthodoxy, according to which there is no salvation
outside the Church. Molière is against blind orthodoxy (as
shown by Orgon and Mme Pernelle) and a rigorous, destructive
interpretation of Christian morality (such as that professed by
Arnolphe in *L'École des Femmes*). His religion is gentle, good,
and human. The cardinal virtues are sincerity and tolerance.

This is in fact a variation of a humanism which had been very much in vogue at the time, and whose disciples were Gassendi and La Mothe le Vayer. We pointed out in the Introduction that Molière may have studied under Gassendi, and La Mothe was among his closest friends.

Since the beginning of the seventeenth century, the 'dévot' had become a definite social type. According to Madame de Sévigné, Molière had one particular man in mind when he wrote *Tartuffe*, a certain abbé Roquette, Bishop of Autun. It is known that this abbé was involved in a scandal similar to the fictitious Tartuffe story in the 1650s, and that he was instrumental in converting Molière's former patron, the Prince de Conty, to a belated bigotry. It is also possible that Molière had in mind the brotherhood known as La Compagnie du Saint Sacrement (popularly called La Cabale des Dévots). This society of severe fanatics, self-appointed watch-dogs of public morals, had become very powerful. In 1660, Mazarin had tried to have the company disbanded.

> Comme la fausse dévotion tient en beaucoup de choses de la vraie, . . . comme les dehors de l'une et de l'autre sont presque tous semblables, il est non seulement aisé, mais d'une suite presque nécessaire, que la même raillerie qui attaque l'une intéresse l'autre, et que les traits dont on peint celle-ci, défigure celle-là, à moins qu'on n'y apporte toutes les précautions d'une charité prudente, exacte et bien intentionnée; ce que le libertinage n'est pas en dis-position de faire. Et voilà, chrétiens, ce qui est arrivé, lorsque des esprits profanes, et bien éloignés de vouloir entrer dans les intérêts de Dieu, ont entrepris de censurer l'hypocrisie, non point pour en réformer l'abus, ce qui n'est pas de leur ressort, mais pour faire une espèce de diversion dont le libertinage pût profiter, en concevant et faisant concevoir d'injustes soupçons de la vraie piété, par de malignes représentations de la fausse. Voilà ce qu'ils ont prétendu, exposant sur le théâtre et à la risée publique un hypocrite imaginaire, ou même, si vous voulez un hypocrite réel, et tournant dans sa personne les choses les

plus saintes en ridicule . . . Voilà ce qu'ils ont affecté, mettant dans la bouche de cet hypocrite des maximes de religion faiblement soutenues, en même temps qu'ils les supposaient fortement attaquées.

(Bourdaloue, during a sermon)

cf. also *l'Onuphre* of La Bruyère (Caractères XIII), and Stendhal, who found the play 'admirable, mais non comique', as did the critic Brunetière:

il m'a semblé que l'impression de *Tartuffe* était décidément d'un drame.

6

Dom Juan

With *Tartuffe* banned from the stage, Molière had quickly to write another play to take its place. He chose as his subject the already often treated legend of the Spanish nobleman, Don Juan de Tenorio, and used it to launch what is in fact an ironic tirade against the hypocrites who had killed *Tartuffe*, by making his hero a self-confessed and unrepentant hypocrite himself. Don Juan's hypocrisy is not part of the legend, and is entirely Molière's invention. Unfortunately, the play shows all the signs of being written hurriedly; it is poorly constructed, there is little or no development or congruity in the characters, and the intrigue, such as it is, (Don Juan's desertion of his wife), has really taken place before the curtain rises on Act 1. Compared with the subtle hypocrisy of Tartuffe, Don Juan is merely a bald liar.

Dom Juan had its first performance on 15 February 1665. It has been suggested that a secret ban was placed on the play by the King immediately after the first night; at any rate, Molière certainly withdrew some of the more blasphemous passages before the second performance. There were fifteen performances in all, well received by the audience, before the play was finally withdrawn, never to appear again in the repertoire in Molière's lifetime. Either prudence or a whispered Royal Command were doubtless responsible. Even after the author's death, his widow commissioned Thomas Corneille to rewrite the play in verse, and it was this plagiarized version which was performed for the next two centuries. The sixteenth performance of Molière's own play was not given at the Comédie Française until 15 January 1847.

A. Dom Juan

1. *Hedonist.* He is selfish to the point of extraordinarily constant egotism. All his actions are designed to achieve only the satisfaction of his own desires; he lives for the moment:

   (*a*) 'Ah! N'allons point songer au mal qui nous peut arriver, et songeons seulement à ce qui nous peut donner du plaisir.' (Act 1, Sc. II)

   One nineteenth-century critic has seen in this selfish hedonism, which he calls 'dilletantism', a fine expression of the instinct of revolt:

   (*b*) 'l'amour artistique du mal, qui n'est qu'un raffinement d'orgueil, la forme la plus savante de l'instinct de révolte.' (Jules Lemaître, *Impressions de Théâtre.* 1888)

2. *Sensualist.* A voluptuary, who does not so much fall in love, as passionately desire to make love. He regards the female as a prey to be caught, conquered, and possessed – then abandoned. His sexual appetite can never find satisfaction.

   (*a*) 'c'est un épouseur à toutes mains.' (Act 1, Sc. I)

   (*b*) 'la constance n'est bonne que pour des ridicules.... Pour moi, la beauté me ravit partout où je la trouve, et je cède facilement à cette douce violence dont elle nous entraine. ... Les inclinations naissantes, après tout, ont des charmes inexplicables, et tout le plaisir de l'amour est dans le changement ... les charmes attrayants d'une conquête à faire.' (Act 1, Sc. II)

   (*c*) 'J'aime la liberté en amour, tu le sais, et je ne saurais me résoudre à renfermer mon coeur entre quatre murailles.' (Act 3, Sc. V)

   Utterly insensitive, he is indifferent to the unhappiness which his egotism may cause others.

3. *Blasphemous.* 'Je crois que deux et deux sont quatre, Sganarelle, et que quatre et quatre sont huit.' (Act 3, Sc. I)

4. *Hypocrite.* A completely unscrupulous machiavellian, Dom

Juan will make any promise, swear to any oath, to satisfy the pleasure of the moment. He admits that he makes a profession of hypocrisy, but claims he is no better nor worse in that than the most respected men of his society. This is the first time that Molière has allowed a bitter tone to creep into his satire, and in the long tirade of Dom Juan parading his hypocrisy, one can sense the fury of the author crying out against his enemies:

(a) L'hypocrisie est un vice à la mode, et tous les vices à la mode passent pour vertus. Le personnage d'homme de bien est le meilleur de tous les personnages qu'on puisse jouer aujourd'hui, et la profession d'hypocrite a de merveilleux avantages. Car c'est un art de qui l'imposture est toujours respectée; et quoi qu'on la découvre, on n'ose rien dire contre elle. Tous les autres vices des hommes sont exposés à la censure, et chacun a la liberté de les attaquer hautement; mais l'hypocrisie est un vice privilégié qui, de sa main, ferme la bouche à tout le monde, et jouit en repos d'une impunité souveraine . . . .

(b) . . . Je m'érigerai en censeur des actions d'autrui, jugerai mal de tout le monde, et n'aurai bonne opinion que de moi . . .

(c) . . . C'est ainsi qu'il faut profiter des faiblesses des hommes, et qu'un sage esprit s'accommode aux vices de son siècle.   (Act 5, Sc. II)

There is only one other speech in the play to counterbalance this exposé of hypocrisy, and that is the tirade of Dom Juan's father, Dom Louis:

(d) Non, non, la naissance n'est rien où la vertu n'est pas. . . . Apprenez enfin qu'un gentilhomme qui vit mal est un monstre dans la nature, que la vertu est le premier titre de noblesse, que je regarde bien moins au nom qu'on signe qu'aux actions qu'on fait . . .   (Act 4, Sc. IV)

One is reminded of a comment by Élise in the later play, *L'Avare*:

Tous les hommes sont semblables par les paroles, et ce n'est que les actions qui les découvrent différents.

B. Sganarelle

1. *His faith.* The familiar insolent servant has a bigger part in this play than in most in which he figures, and is given the job of trying to persuade Dom Juan to mend his ways. His Christianity is a very naïve, ludicrous form of deism, which would have little chance of shaking an atheist:

> (*a*) je comprends fort bien que ce monde que nous voyons n'est pas un champignon qui soit venu tout seul en une nuit.   (Act 3, Sc. I)

Sganarelle's faith is founded on the most idiotic superstition. 'Il met sur le même plan l'Enfer, le Ciel et le loup-garou.'
>   (R. Jasinski: *Molière*)

2. *His morals.* Sganarelle's frequent bouts of moralizing are no less inarticulate, and one cannot but agree with Dom Juan when he refers to 'tes sottes moralités'.

> (*a*) les bonnes préceptes valent mieux que les belles paroles; les belles paroles se trouvent à la cour; etc., etc.
>   (Act 5, Sc. II)

> (*b*) une méchante vie amène une méchante mort.
>   (Act 1, Sc. II)

C. Molière's Intention

Is the play anti-Christian, or is it not? First and foremost it is a comedy, and there is much comic invention in the scenes between Dom Juan and Sganarelle, and when Dom Juan is with the two peasant girls to whom he has promised betrothal. But it is impossible to deny a far more serious content to this play. We have already drawn attention to the aspect of personal vendetta, of Molière's frustrated cry of contempt for the religious hypocrites who had forced *Tartuffe* off the stage. At least one contemporary, however, saw in *Dom Juan* an undisguised mockery of religion:

> Qui peut supporter la hardiesse d'un farceur qui fait plaisanterie de la religion, qui tient école du libertinage,

et qui rend la majesté de Dieu le jouet d'un maître et d'un valet de théâtre, d'un athée qui s'en rit, et d'un valet, plus impie que son maître, qui en fait rire les autres? . . . Une religieuse débauchée, et dont l'on publie la prostitution; un pauvre à qui l'on donne l'aumône à condition de renier Dieu; un libertin qui séduit autant de filles qu'il en rencontre; un enfant qui se moque de son père et qui souhaite sa mort.'   (le Sieur de Rochement, 1665)

All this is true, and all these passages referred to by Rochemont do shock on first reading. But it might be pointed out that Dom Juan is paid for his sins by celestial intervention in the last minutes of the play, when he is swallowed for ever into the ground. Jasinski thinks that this dénouement alone shows that Molière condemns Dom Juan and punishes him accordingly. Ergo, the play is not blasphemous. But Michelet has claimed that, since the villain does not repent before his disappearance, and dies as sinful as he lived, there can be no moral effect in this dénouement. It is perhaps also significant that Sganarelle, who is given the task of defending the precepts of the Church against Dom Juan's persuasive atheism, and who does so with singular ineffectiveness and the most absurd lack of reasoning, was played originally by Molière himself.

We shall pass over the next play in chronological order, *L'Amour Médecin*, (15 September 1665), a pleasant comedy without weight or purpose, since superseded by Molière's other, more thoughtful, plays whose subject was also to be the medical profession.

With *Tartuffe* banned from the stage, and *Dom Juan* withdrawn after only fifteen performances, and literary as well as personal enemies hunting him down mercilessly for several years now, Molière had every reason to feel bitter resentment against society in general. It seemed that no efforts of his could bring tolerance and understanding to the minds of thoughtless people. Polite Society was always more powerful than he. So he turned his wrath upon Polite Society, and wrote *Le Misanthrope*, first performed on 4 June 1666.

7

Le Misanthrope

More subtle than anything Molière had previously written, or was subsequently to write, *Le Misanthrope* did not find immediate favour with a public which had come to expect more overtly controversial and provocative plays from him. After the first three performances, the audience became smaller and smaller, until the play had to be taken from the repertory for long periods at a time, for financial reasons. It was, however, recognized by contemporaries as a masterpiece.

A. Alceste

1. L'Atrabilaire

Molière subtitles his play 'L'Atrabilaire Amoureux'. Alceste is first and foremost a pessimist, disgusted with the pettiness of daily human intercourse and the treachery of human nature, at war with society. He likes to contradict and to reproach; he always says what he thinks, and will not retract an honestly held opinion. He has nothing but contempt for contemporary fashions in literature, manners or clothing, but sets instead a high value on the real man beneath social superficialities and pretences. This appears particularly in the nature of his love for Célimène, and the way he chooses to express it. His passionate outbursts to her in a salon where the custom is to be polite, and hence as unspontaneous as it is possible to be, appear grotesque in those circumstances.

According to Antoine Adam:

> 'son envers fâcheux, c'est qu'il a l'esprit contrariant. Il penserait se manquer à soi-même s'il se rangeait à l'avis

de quelqu'un. Il n'admet pas qu'on le blâme, ni qu'on le loue.'

(a) Et ne faut-il pas bien que monsieur contredise?
(Célimène, Act 2, Sc. IV)

2. L'Orgueilleux

Alceste is proud enough to want to be set apart from other men, to be admired for his frankness and honesty; there is almost a death-wish in his furious insistence on being victimized for his principles; he is glad that Oronte should drag him to court for his insult, and even more glad, one might say, that the verdict should be against himself. This only confirms him in his proud pessimism, and demonstrates to the world that he is right. One clue to his character is the simple compulsion always to have the last word, no matter what. 'N'accordant rien aux préjugés du monde, il va hardiment son chemin sans se soucier du qu'en-dira-t-on.' (Sarcey.) The word 'moi' is for ever on his mouth; it is significantly almost the first word which Molière has him say after his first entrance:

(a) Moi, je veux me fâcher, et je ne veux point entendre.
(Act 1, Sc. I)

When he is finally face to face with Célimène, alone, he takes the opportunity to launch into a long philosophical soliloquy (Act 4, Scene III). And the one line which reveals better than any other his stubborn pride in being different comes during the famous sonnet scene:

(b) C'est qu'ils ont l'art de feindre, et moi, je ne l'ai pas.

3. Le Vertueux

(a) C'est une vertu rare au siècle d'aujourd'hui.
(Éliante, Act 4, Sc. I)

One has the impression that Alceste is for ever cultivating his virtue and drawing attention to it, in order to give himself the right to despise the world. This virtue is in some measure a subtle form of vanity.

> (b) Je veux qu'on soit sincère, et qu'en homme d'honneur
> On ne lâche aucun mot qui ne parte du coeur.
>
> (Act 1, Sc. I)

There is also a certain naïvety in this belief that sincerity should give him the right to all he desires.

4. Son humeur noire

According to Antoine Adam, he is 'ni grondeur, ni bourru.' He is melancholy, sullen, too easily hurt, hypersensitive. He says he wants to hide in 'ce petit coin sombre avec mon noir chagrin'. It is in moments like this that we discern the depth of his misanthropy. He does, in fact, hate mankind:

> 'les uns parce qu'ils sont méchants et malfaisants et les autres pour être aux méchants complaisants.'

He goes so far as to say that he wants to 'se tirer du commerce des hommes.'

5. Is he an 'honnête homme'?

No. On the contrary, he conforms in no way to the ideal of the 'honnête homme' which appears in so much of the literature of the seventeenth century; he is the arch non-conformist. In the words of La Rochefoucauld, an 'honnête homme' was 'celui qui ne se pique de rien.' This could certainly not be said of Alceste.

6. Is he ridiculous?

In the words of Célimène, Alceste is a 'grand extravagant'. But does this make him an object of ridicule and a real subject for comedy? Daniel Mornet's view is that Alceste is not ridiculous for his moral rectitude, but for his exaggerated way of showing it. He takes everything too seriously and solemnly, and he habitually makes mountains out of molehills. For instance,

Alceste thinks, and says, that it is contemptible hypocrisy to kiss a man on the cheek in a salon unless you know him very well indeed; Mornet says this is absurd, since such an embrace would correspond to our shaking hands with a stranger at a party.

Antoine Adam does not agree. He admits that effusive greetings were then the rule in polite society, but claims that Molière is, through Alceste, satirizing such customs which he abhors, particularly when they become so mannered, so studied, exaggerated and therefore meaningless. Alceste is, then, emphatically *not* ridiculous in protesting against the abuse of social intercourse; he is, in this respect at least, Molière's mouthpiece.

Neither is he ridiculous in being such a harsh critic of Oronte's sonnet:

> Ce n'est que jeux de mots, qu'affectation pure,
> Et ce n'est point ainsi que parle la nature.
> Le méchant goût du siècle en cela me fait peur.

Here again, Alceste is clearly speaking on behalf of Molière.

So, because he is sullen, bitter, melancholy, rather than violent (like Harpagon in *L'Avare* and Arnolphe in *L'École des Femmes*), he is not really a ridiculous character. The comedy of the part lies rather in the situations in which he finds himself as a logical result of being true to himself.

It is also significant, and another element in the comedy, that he is afraid of being made a fool of by the one person he adores, Célimène (cf. Arnolphe). This goes some way towards explaining his intransigent attitude towards her.

The question as to whether or not Alceste is a comic character has been debated by scholars for nearly three hundred years, and the debate continues. One eminent author is particularly responsible for the idea that the character is comic, and therefore incongruous, and that is Jean-Jacques Rousseau:

> Vous ne sauriez me nier deux choses: qu'Alceste, dans cette pièce, est un homme droit, sincère, estimable, un

véritable homme de bien; l'autre, que l'auteur lui donne
un personnage ridicule . . . Dans toutes les autres pièces
de Molière, le personnage ridicule est haïssable ou mépris-
able. Dans celle-là, quoique Alceste ait des défauts réels
dont on n'a pas tort de rire, on sent pourtant au fond du
cœur un respect pour lui dont on ne peut se défendre.
(Rousseau, *Lettre à d'Alembert*, 1758)

However, Molière rarely leaves a question of interpretation
unanswered. One only has to go to his text or his prefaces to
find a fairly explicit analysis of his intentions. There are some
lines in *La Critique de l'École des Femmes*, spoken by Dorante,
which are apt at this point:

il n'est pas incompatible qu'une personne soit ridicule en
de certaines choses et honnête homme en d'autres.

Finally, it is of course ludicrous to consider Alceste as the
first 'homme absurde', as some modern commentators have
suggested, rising in rebellion against the injustice of the human
condition. Alceste is not a philosopher, but an unhappy, dis-
couraged and embittered man. He finally retreats into loneli-
ness.

B. Célimène

She is above all, 'une coquette'. Though only twenty years old,
she has grace, elegance, wit, and a youthful desire to enjoy life
to the full. Life, of course, for a pretty, intelligent girl of her
age and class, includes being courted, flattered and adored by
men. She is afraid of being alone, and her gay extrovertism
contrasts neatly with Alceste's brooding introspection.

1. La solitude effraye une âme de vingt ans.
(Act 5, Sc. IV)

2. Moi, renoncer au monde avant que de vieillir?   (idem)

She is incapable of returning Alceste's deep and sincere love.
For Célimène, love is only a game; she has no doubt been
nourished in her teens on the 'précieux' novels which are so

much in vogue, and is probably acquainted with La Carte du Tendre (see Chapter 2: *Les Précieuses Ridicules*). If Alceste does not know the rules of the game, so much the worse for him! Words of love from Célimène are mere pawns in the ritual of gallantry. How can I be sure that you love me, asks Alceste. She replies, true to the copy-book, and with an impish smile which must exasperate him:

> 3. Je pense qu'ayant pris le soin de vous le dire
>   Un aveu de la sorte a de quoi vous suffire.
>
> (Act 2, Sc. I)

She in turn is exasperated by Alceste's jealous rages and monumental sincerity, which are too embarrassingly real in her world of social illusions, and she finally cries petulantly:

> 4. Non, vous ne m'aimez pas comme il faut que l'on aime.
>
> (Act 4, Sc. III)

(It is worth pausing to note here that some critics have interpreted this line quite differently, and have seen it as a cry of truth from a perspicacious young woman who has understood that Alceste is incapable of loving anyone but himself.)

Célimène also has a wicked tongue, which is evident in the *scène des portraits*, and in the exquisite scene with Arsinoé, in which she destroys the latter's veiled insults with beautifully timed and phrased thrusts of her own.

Daniel Mornet (who is always at pains to interpret the plays in the light of their seventeenth-century background) claims that she is not guilty of any dishonour, and that Alceste is wrong to castigate her so cruelly. In the seventeenth century (he says), the sort of letters which Célimène has written and which are the cause of her quarrel and final rupture with Alceste did not commit the writer in any way. The letter was then a form of literature, or at least a harmless social amusement; the writer sought to be amusing, clever or witty, but not sincere. This may well be so, but it does not annul the validity of Alceste's (and Molière's) protest against such a social 'amusement'.

C. Philinte

1. Mais quand on est du monde, il faut bien que l'on rende
   Quelques dehors civils que l'usage demande.

2. Il est bien des endroits où la pleine franchise
   Deviendrait ridicule et serait peu permise.

3. Faisons un peu de grâce à la nature humaine.

4. Il faut, parmi le monde, une vertu traitable.

5. La parfaite raison fuit toute extrémité
   Et veut que l'on soit sage avec sobriété.

6. Et c'est une folie à nulle autre seconde
   De vouloir se mêler de corriger le monde.

7. Le monde par vos soins ne changera pas.

8. Mon phlegme est philosophe autant que votre bile.

This is the language of 'gassendisme', a philosophical school under Gassendi which had opposed the Cartesian rationalism, and which represents, in the opinion of many scholars, the philosophy of Molière himself.

Is Philinte in fact Molière's mouthpiece, or not? Or is it rather Alceste? The question has been the subject of much debate. In a way, Molière is both Alceste and Philinte; the play is a sort of dialogue between Molière as he is, and Molière as he would like to be, or between the Molière in society, and the Molière who is detached from it, and observes the human drama from outside. These are interesting speculations, but in the last resort it is both pointless and fruitless to try to identify the author with any of his characters, in the absence of any definite indication from him.

Unlike Alceste, Philinte is an 'honnête homme', loyal, reasonable, and not complacent. The lies of which Alceste accuses him are merely the unimportant half-truths which social politeness demands, and which few civilized people can avoid:

> L'ami du Misanthrope est si raisonnable que tout le monde devrait l'imiter; il n'est ni trop, ni trop peu critique.
>
> (Donneau de Visé)

Philinte provides an admirable contrast with Alceste. He knows that one must not expect too much from life, that one must learn to live with one's ideals for ever unsatisfied.

D. Arsinoé

Arsinoé is essentially false, a hypocrite in everything she says. Molière seems to have more contempt for prudes than for almost any other social type which he derides, more than the 'précieuses', the marquesses, the doctors. Célimène sums her up in two lines:

> Elle tâche à couvrir d'un faux voile de prude
> Ce que chez elle on voit d'affreuse solitude.

In her famous quarrel scene with Célimène, Arsinoé loses ignominiously. She is reduced to a helpless splutter by the biting wit of this young woman whose every sentence is a dagger. What more cruel reflection than Célimène's, when she says that 'il y a une saison pour la galanterie, et une autre pour la pruderie.'

In her scene with Alceste, Arsinoé loses again. She is in love with him, but is too frightened to admit it, because she realizes she would be refused. She therefore lies her way through the whole interview. At her entry, she is at pains to establish that *she* doesn't want to see him, but comes only at the request of Célimène, who 'veut que je vous entretienne'. To win him over, she tries first flattery, then promises to use her influence in his favour. Both manœuvres fail, and if she knew Alceste better, she wouldn't have attempted either of them.

E. Oronte, Acaste, Clitandre, Éliante

Oronte's only crimes are to be a bad poet, and to be vain. He believes that his nobility presupposes a creative talent. He is not nearly so ridiculous as Mascarille (in *Les Précieuses Ridicules*), or Trissotin (in *Les Femmes Savantes*), who is despicable as well as silly. Oronte, on the other hand, is courteous and likeable, if only he wouldn't put pen to paper. Acaste and Clitandre are two of the foppish marquesses who adorn much of Molière's work. They are extremely vain, silly, and conceited. They are:

> Ces obligeants diseurs d'inutiles paroles.

The sincere and charitable Éliante conforms to Alceste's ideal. She refuses to take part in the fashionable Portrait Game, which she considers unkind. Moreover, she does not get angry when Alceste clumsily and tactlessly offers her his love, when he has been refused by Célimène, in spite of the fact that she both admires him, and likes him.

She and Alceste appear to agree in their ideas about love, and yet Éliante is, if anything, more perspicacious on the subject than even he:

1. Mais la raison n'est pas ce qui règle l'amour. (Alceste)

2. . . . dans l'object aimé tout leur devient aimable.
   Ils comptent les défauts pour des perfections. (Éliante)

If Éliante is right, then perhaps Alceste is not really in love with Célimène at all, since, far from failing to recognize her faults, he is very conscious of them, even exaggerates them, and seems to take a pleasure in exaggerating them. The truth lies somewhere in between. His intelligence teaches him to beware of Célimène, who cannot answer his ideal, but his heart is unable to listen. Molière seems to share some of the bitterness of Proust. Does not Swann's love for Odette echo the imprisoning love which Alceste has for Célimène?

The Critics' Verdict

It has been suggested that *Le Misanthrope* is not strictly a play at all, because it is devoid of action. The first to maintain this point of view was Schlegel, who complained that the play dragged monotonously from one conversation to another; he saw it as a mere succession of philosophical arguments. Hémon qualified this harsh judgement by saying that all the action took place in Alceste's mind, and Copeau simplified the matter even further with his view that the action was about a man who strove to 'get through' to a woman, but never succeeded. All of these criticisms are unworthy of Molière. It was his friend and contemporary, Donneau de Visé, who wrote the most intelligent comment on the subject of action in *Le Misanthrope*, and the comment happens to accord with Molière's own declared intentions as a dramatist:

> Il n'a point voulu faire une comédie pleine d'incidents, mais une pièce, seulement, où il pût parler contre les mœurs du siècle.
> (Donneau de Visé, *Lettre sur Le Misanthrope*)

Antoine Adam, nearly 300 years later, developed this idea and added his own personal note:

> Molière sait qu'il a contre lui tous ceux qui mentent et qui trichent, les pédants, ceux qu'il a nommés un jour les faux-monnayeurs. Pour réussir dans la société, il faut être complaisant, il faut à chaque instant trahir sa pensée, flatter les puissants, cultiver les influences. On devine dans le Misanthrope un homme qui perd patience et qui sent le besoin de crier sa colère.

It is because he wanted to draw a 'portrait du siècle' that Molière chose, for the first time, to write a play about high society, and to place a congenital pessimist in the middle of it. The juxtaposition of an honest, plain-speaking, self-confessed hater of mankind on the one hand, and a troup of vain noblemen, a flirt, and a prude on the other, served the purpose admirably. Yet, contrary to Schlegel's criticism, he did not make a treatise out of his play. As Donneau de Visé points out:

> il laisse partout deviner plus qu'il ne dit.

Adam develops another interesting idea, according to which *Le Misanthrope* is not only a satire of high society, but a satire of its own author. (pp. 348 et seq.) Jasinski agrees, and makes the valid point that the faithful and knowledgeable La Grange had no doubt the subject of the play was taken from Molière's domestic life. Who was in a better position to know? In this event, Alceste would be Molière, and Célimène would be his exasperatingly flirtatious wife Armande. 'La source principle du *Misanthrope* doit être cherchée dans la vie de Molière.' (R. Jasinski, op cit., p. 153.)

Finally, is this comedy a 'tragedy'? It certainly ends on an unhappy note, 'le tragique des espoirs brisés' (Jasinski), but this is not enough to tag the word tragedy on to an exceedingly amusing play. On the other hand, Molière does avoid the more obvious comic resources, and prefers to provoke, in this case, more of an intellectual amusement than a bawdy laugh. As de Visé puts it, the comic aspects 'font continuellement rire dans l'âme.'

8

L'Avare

In the little more than two years which separate *Le Misanthrope* from *L'Avare*, Molière wrote three plays, *Le Médecin Malgré Lui*, *Amphitryon* and *Georges Dandin*, plus two short entertainments for the Court of Louis XIV. Then, *L'Avare* opened on 9 September 1668, with Molière in the role of Harpagon.

1. Harpagon

> Ce vieillard, physiquement épuisé, moralement traqué, est un bouffon. Bouffon devant Marianne, bouffon dans ses pauvres colères, bouffon dans sa naiveté lorsqu'il boit les flatteries de Frosine. Ce tyran est seulement ridicule.
>
> (Antoine Adam)

Adam's view quoted above is essentially a rejection of the widely-held opinion that Harpagon is a grotesque and despicable character, and that *L'Avare* is therefore a tragedy. Goethe was the first, and most famous, supporter of this interpretation, which is not entirely without foundation, and it is as well that we should examine first what evidence there is in the play to support the view that Harpagon is a tyrant rather than a fool.

There is certainly something repugnant in his declared love for a girl young enough to be his daughter, in the passion for money which stifles all his natural paternal affection and corrupts his moral sense. At one point, after Valère has saved Élise, Harpagon's daughter, from drowning, and she is reduced to imploring her father on bended knees not to 'pousser les choses dans les dernières violences du pouvoir paternel', he goes as far as to say that Valère would have done better, from his point of view, to let her drown. Also, like Orgon in *Tartuffe*, he disinherits his son and lays his curse upon him, to which Cléante replies contemptuously, 'Je n'ai que faire de vos dons!' Not a very happy household, certainly. Harpagon is:

de tous les humains l'humain le moins humain, le mortel de tous les mortels le plus dur et le plus serré.

But, as Émile Faguet justly notes, Harpagon is drawn, like many of Molière's central characters, at once odious and ridiculous, and it is the ridiculous side of his nature which is most important.

Although he tries hard to be tyrannical, he is physically incapable of frightening anyone, and succeeds only in being a laughing-stock:

la fable et la risée de tout le monde.

He sacrifices honour and reputation 'au désir insatiable d'entasser écu sur écu', and 'il aime l'argent plus que réputation, qu'honneur et que vertu, et la vue d'un demandeur lui donne des convulsions.' There is the famous line which Molière gives to La Flèche, 'donner est un mot pour qui il a tant d'aversion qu'il ne dit jamais je vous donne, mais je vous prête le bonjour.' His moneybox has become 'mon support, ma consolation, ma joie'. In the last resort, however 'tragic' may be his condition, we are moved to laughter rather than tears by his absurd exaggerations.

Like Arnolphe (in *L'Écoles des Femmes*), Harpagon is very suspicious and distrustful. There is a reference to 'les soupçons de son esprit malade', in his very first scene with La Flèche, when he insists on searching the poor servant. He is also a liar and a hypocrite, tormented with worries, and enjoying it.

He shows himself to be incredibly stupid when Marianne and Cléante can exchange words of love in his presence without his catching on (Act 3, Scene VII). This in spite of his avowed distrust of other people. Indeed, he is so naïve as to believe Frosine's word, when she tells him that Marianne prefers old men and cannot stand the sight of a young man.

Like M. Jourdain (in *Le Bourgeois Gentilhomme*), he is extremely clumsy in love. The best image of flattery which he can conjure up to seduce Marianne is to tell her that she is 'le plus bel astre dans le ciel des astres.'

The real comedy in this character lies in the enormous gulf which exists between Harpagon as he sees himself, and Harpagon as we see him. He is terrified of being made a fool of, and is made a fool of constantly.

2. Valère

il faut manger pour vivre et non pas vivre pour manger.

Valère is little more than a rather colourless romantic hero, with occasional flashes of good sense. His defence of flattery recalls many of Philinte's speeches in *Le Misanthrope*:

ce n'est pas la faute de ceux qui flattent, mais de ceux qui veulent être flattés.   (Valère, Act 1, Sc. I)

3. Cléante, Élise, Marianne

These three characters exist only for love, and are not allowed to develop any real personality. They are perfect contrasts to Harpagon, since they represent all the humility, the humour, the sincerity and the honesty which he lacks. It is interesting to note the 'précieux' style of many of Cléante's speeches.

4. Maître Jacques, Frosine, La Flèche

All three are true to the tradition of Molière's servants, though less colourful than most. They are on the side of the young lovers against the whims of the foolish old man. Maître Jacques is more devoted to his horses than his master.

5. Love

Hélas, qu'avec facilité on se laisse persuader par les personnes que l'on aime.   (Élise, Act 1, Sc. I)

6. Marriage and Paternal Authority

Valère has some pertinent things to say about the importance of marriage in the famous 'sans dot' scene:

le mariage est une plus grande affaire qu'on ne peut croire; qu'il y va d'être heureux ou malheureux toute sa vie, et qu'un engagement qui doit durer jusqu'à la mort ne se doit jamais faire qu'avec de grandes précautions.

(Act 1, Sc. V)

And in another scene, Cléante is equally frank on the subject with his father:

HARP: Ne suis-je pas ton père, et ne me dois-tu pas respect?
CLÉ: Ce ne sont point ici des choses où les enfants soient obligés de déférer aux pères, et l'amour ne connaît personne.

It is reasonable to infer, especially in conjunction with other pronouncements on the same subject in different plays, that these are expressions of Molière's own view.

7. The Author's Intentions

Molière wanted to present a picture of the misfortunes caused by greed and avarice, but Harpagon is not, as Gustave Lanson has maintained, a mere abstraction, a picture of The Universal Miser. He is very much a character in his own right, with his own personality and foibles.

The play is just as much about tender young love as it is about avarice, and it is in the scenes involving the four lovers that Molière has the most important and revealing things to say. His own tenderness towards young lovers, and his anger with any aspect of society which conspires to frustrate them, are apparent. The first two scenes of the first act are devoted to displaying the happiness of the four lovers. It is only in the third scene that this happiness is threatened by Harpagon's entrance, already prepared in Cléante's words:

> Voilà où les jeunes gens sont réduits par la maudite avarice des pères.

If there is any moral in the play, it lies in these lines of Cléante. Molière appreciates the naïvety, the generosity, the innocence of youth, and abhors the destruction of idealism by unreasonable parents. Of course, adolescents should respect their parents, if these parents are sane and reasonable. If they are not, Molière is unhesitatingly on the side of the adolescents.

9

Le Bourgeois Gentilhomme

Le Bourgeois Gentilhomme was something of an innovation, in that it represented a collaboration between Molière and Lully to produce an entertainment which had as much music and dancing in it as acting. As such, it is as important for the history of ballet as it is for the study of seventeenth-century French drama, if not more so. Louis XIV was accounted a very good dancer himself, and did much to encourage the development of ballet, though in a form which bears little resemblance to what we see at Covent Garden in the twentieth century.

This 'comédie-ballet' was presented to the Court on 14 October 1670, and later that same year to the general Parisian public. The immediate success of the play contrasted with the poor reception accorded to *L'Avare* at the first performances.

1. Monsieur Jourdain

A. Vain

The vanity of M. Jourdain is the vanity of the newly rich, whom money has enabled to climb the social ladder. He loves to display the spoils which his sudden wealth has bought, to call his lackeys from time to time, for the sheer joy of having them run to him; he is terribly proud of his rich wardrobe, of the teachers whom he has employed, of the very fact that the world seems to be revolving around him, and that everybody is busy satisfying his whims and fancies.

However, his desire to imitate 'les gens de qualité', innocent enough in itself, has become an absurd obsession which blinds him to the cunning manœuvres of Dorante and to the subservient flattery of his teachers, and reduces him to a laughable 'fantoche':

> ... et surtout ayez soin tous deux de marcher immédiate-ment sur mes pas, afin qu'on voie bien vous êtes à moi.

B. Naïve

His natural naïvety is rendered incurable by 'les visions de noblesse et de galanterie qu'il est allé se mettre en tête.' He trusts everyone. M. Jourdain asks how one should greet a marchioness, and takes seriously the perfectly ludicrous reply; not only that, he tries it out! It is very easy to take advantage of his ignorance, simply by appealing to his incipient snobbery. When he is told that 'gens de qualité' wear the flowers upside-down on their coats, he immediately gives instructions to his tailor that his coat should so be redesigned.

C. Clumsy

As Harpagon (in *L'Avare*) made a fool of himself when trying to declare love for Marianne, so M. Jourdain shows himself to be a very poor, and very amusing, potential lover of the marchioness:

> me voir assez fortuné pour être si heureux que d'avoir le bonheur que vous ayez eu la bonté de m'accorder la grâce de me faire l'honneur de m'honorer de la faveur de votre présence, etc.

This lamentable declaration is in fact a very clever satire on the style of language so commonly used in the interminable précieux novels of the period.

M. Jourdain is not really in love with Dorimène, of course. It would, however, flatter his vanity and his idea of his position in society if she were to be in love with him. That's all.

D. Timid

Il est timide en face des gens du monde, s'efforçant avec

une insigne maladresse d'imiter leurs usages, étalant sa
richesse pour masquer ce sentiment d'infériorité qu'il
n'arrive pas à étouffer.   (Antoine Adam)

E. Ignorant

The ignorance of M. Jourdain is more profound than one would
dare imagine. He is, certainly, obsessed with a desire to gain
more knowledge. Jean-Jacques Rousseau found this a highly
commendable trait in his character, and reproached Molière for
making fun of it. But Rousseau misses the point. Jourdain wants
to appear more intelligent simply in order to impress, and to
hold his own with his beloved 'gens de qualité'. The shallowness
of his quest for knowledge and scholarship is very soon apparent:

(*a*) Apprenons autre chose qui soit plus joli.
(*b*) Par ma foi! il y a plus de quarante ans que je dis de la
      prose sans que je n'en susse rien.
(*c*) Belle marquise, vos beaux yeux me font mourir d'amour.

And yet, beneath the absurd postures, Monsieur Jourdain
remains likeable. There is little bitterness in the portrait of this
foolish but basically decent man.

2. Madame Jourdain

Madame Jourdain is, like her husband, of bourgeois stock, but
unlike her husband, is content to remain so. She expresses herself with very down-to-earth language, completely shorn of the
elegant pretensions which her husband is trying hard to culti-
vate. She has a very sure idea of what is right and what is wrong,
dictated not by learning, but by sheer common sense, and experience; she is also very witty, and without her, Molière's play
would be much the poorer.

(*a*) Comment se porte-t-elle?
      Elle se porte sur ses deux jambes.
(*b*) Il y a longtemps que je sens les choses, et je ne suis pas
      une bête.

(c) Oui, il a des bontés pour vous, et vous fait des caresses, mais il vous emprunte votre argent.

(d) Cet homme-là fait de vous une vache à lait.

(e) Les alliances avec plus grand que soi sont sujettes toujours à de fâcheux inconvénients. Je ne veux point qu'un gendre puisse à ma fille reprocher ses parents, et qu'elle ait des enfants qui aient honte de m'appeler leur grand'maman . . . je veux un homme, en un mot, qui m'ait obligation de ma fille, et à qui je puisse dire: 'Mettez-vous là, mon gendre, et dinez avec moi.'

3. Nicole

She exists really as support for Madame Jourdain, whose frankness she shares, and with whom she joins forces to make her master realize he is making a fool of himself. She 'se fourre toujours dans la conversation', and has a value as a comic personality in her own right. She is perhaps the most persistent, stubborn, and cheeky of all Molière's insubordinate servants:

Tenez, monsieur, battez-moi plutôt, et me laissez rire tout mon soûl, cela me fera plus de bien.

4. Cléonte

Cléonte and Lucile, the two lovers, do not appear until the sixth scene of the third act. They have no particular interest, apart from being essential to one of the themes, but Cléonte has one scene in which there is a speech so serious, so earnest in its tone, and so much in accord with what we have so far been able to discover of Molière's view of life from his earlier plays, that one is forced into the conclusion that, at this point, the author allowed himself to speak through a secondary character in his play. It is questionable whether the audience would notice the insertion even today:

Je trouve que toute imposture est indigne d'un honnête homme, et qu'il y a de la lâcheté à déguiser ce que le Ciel nous a fait naître, à se parer aux yeux du monde d'un titre dérobé, à se vouloir donner pour ce qu'on n'est pas.

A description which applies not only to M. Jourdain, but with equal validity to Arsinoé (in *Le Misanthrope*), Tartuffe (in *Tartuffe*), Arnolphe (in *L'École des Femmes*), and the many other 'faux-monnayeurs' in Molière's work.

5. Other Characters

Covielle is rather like La Flèche (in *L'Avare*) and Scapin (in *Les Fourberies de Scapin*), devoted to his master, but clever and unscrupulous when it comes to making a fool of M. Jourdain.

Dorante is machiavellian, cast in the same mould as Tartuffe and Trissotin (in *Les Femmes Savantes*). And yet, Molière turns him, clearly for expedient reasons, from an odious scheming nobleman into a perfectly likeable man, at the end of the play. The change is quite incongruous, and unexplained.

The philosophy teacher is, in a way, a caricature of all the 'raisonneurs' in the plays (Philinte in *Le Misanthrope*, Chrysalde in *L'École des Femmes*, etc.), but unlike them, he can rarely practice what he preaches:

> Un homme sage est au-dessus de toutes les injures qu'on peut lui dire; et la grande réponse qu'on doit faire aux outrages, c'est la modération et la patience.

6. The Author's Intentions

(*a*) The intrigue, or plot, is the same as in many other works by Molière: the obsessions of a father sow dissension in the household and threaten to destroy the happiness of his daughter, whom he wants to marry against her wishes.

(*b*) In fact, there is no plot at all until the third act, the first two acts being little more than a series of 'lazzi'. When the story does get under way, it is extremely improbable. One must remember that the play was largely subordinate to the ballet, and only existed in order to build up towards the very elaborate ballet sequence at the end, the lunatic Turkish Ceremony.

(*c*) And yet, in spite of these shortcomings, and in spite of the fact that he was writing a 'comédie-ballet', Molière transformed what might have been an empty entertainment into a social study of contemporary snobbery.

(d) Antoine Adam claims that the 'mamamouchi' ceremony at the end is meant to be a parody of religious rites. It seems to us that this is indulging a desire for interpretation a little too generously. On the contrary, the ceremony is clearly meant to make fun of Turkish, not Christian, rites. A Turkish envoy was in Paris at the time, and was the object of much popular derision.

(e) It has also been suggested that the whole play is a satire on Colbert, whose vulgarity and snobbery were well-known. This is very likely true.[1]

On 24 May 1671, Molière presented his *Les Fourberies de Scapin*, a straightforward, unpretentious farce, which is still enormously popular in the repertory of the Comédie Française, and deservedly so. Although one of the most delightful of all farces, it is almost devoid of social comment (as one would expect it to be), and does not therefore lend itself easily to analysis. Let it only be said that Boileau's pedantic dismissal of the work as being unworthy of its author was silly and un-necessary:

> Dans ce sac ridicule où Scapin s'enveloppe
> Je ne reconnais plus l'auteur du *Misanthrope*.

A few months later there appeared another play, *La Comtesse d'Escarbagnas*, not very noteworthy, and then, in 1672, *Les Femmes Savantes*.

[1] See J. Marion, *Molière a-t-il Songé à Colbert?* in Revue Hist. Litt., April – June 1938.

10

Les Femmes Savantes

1. Philaminte

Authoritarian, bossy, with a masculine determination to have things done her way, to be mistress of her household, and to hold her place in society. In her desire to rule the roost, she all but eclipses her poor husband, Chrysale, and reduces him to the status of a servant.

> Je ne veux point d'obstacle aux désirs que je montre,

she says, and one is bound to believe her. Selfishness and a blind obsession with her social rating have stifled all maternal love, and all femininity.

Philaminte is very vain. She wants to marry her daughter Henriette to the poet Trissotin, not to further her daughter's happiness, not even because such a marriage, though empty of love, would be useful to Henriette in society (which is the excuse she gives most often), but to satisfy her own vanity. She rather likes the idea of having a celebrated wit and poet for a son-in-law. ('Ce n'est pas *mon* compte de souffrir dans *mon* sang une pareille honte.') Every consideration must be subordinate to the indulgence of her massive egoism.

She is not exactly 'précieuse' as Cathos and Magdelon were in *Les Précieuses Ridicules*, at least not in the restricted sense which the word carried in the years following 1650. Of course, this play was composed some thirteen years after *Les Précieuses Ridicules*, when the principals of Préciosité had been further vulgarized and exaggerated. It had become synonymous with pseudo-intellectualism of the most vapid and pretentious kind.

Philaminte does speak like a précieuse, attaching a great importance to matters of grammar and syntax ('un mot sauvage et bas'), but her most earnest desire is to demonstrate that women may hold their own in a man's world, and shine equally with their husbands in the arts and sciences ('que de science aussi les femmes sont meublées'). This is not an unworthy ambition in itself, but Philaminte pushes the principle to absurd extremes, and therein lies the comedy. Her plans are grandiose and pretentious; she would like nothing better than to be famous.

However, Philaminte is not altogether a fool. She is fundamentally an intelligent woman, and when she discovers Trissotin's cupidity in Act 5, and her own attendant financial ruin, she displays a calm, stoic resignation which does her credit. Her loudly heralded philosophy is not, therefore, a mere matter of words. This (to us) sudden change in character endears her to the audience somewhat, at the last moment, and compromises the coherence of the character.

2. Armande

Armande, the elder daughter, is selfish like her mother, and extremely disrespectful towards her father, whom she openly despises.

She is, in fact, one of Molière's most subtle and closely drawn characters. We learn from the text that she had been beautiful in her youth, and had been secretly in love with Clitandre. She still loves him, but having resisted his most innocent advances out of prudery, conceit, and a *Précieuse* concern for gallant courtship, she now sees him falling in love with her pretty young sister. She is tormented with a bitter jealousy, which she tries in vain to conceal beneath a cloak of pompous self-righteousness. The very idea of children fills her with hypocritical disgust; she speaks of dirty passions, and echoing a cardinal precept of the Précieuses (see Chapter 2), claims that her ideal is a marriage in which bodily pleasures are banished:

(a) d'un idole d'époux et des marmots d'enfants.
(b) sales désirs.
(c) Cette union des coeurs où les corps n'entrent pas.

It is easy to see that this sexless idealism is false, the crippled product of self-imposed abstention by a good-looking woman who is really very highly sexed. She lies to herself even more than she lies to others. One might almost type Armande as a female version of Tartuffe, except that Tartuffe remained conscious of his hypocrisy, which he used in a machiavellian way, whereas for Armande, hypocrisy has become a way of life, the sublimation of an unhappy woman.

Occasionally, the desires show through. In the very first scene of the play, she says that, although her passions are governed by her reason, she does not altogether renounce 'les douceurs des encens', a very sensuous and revealing phrase. The sentiment reminds one of Tartuffe's famous

Pour être dévot, je ne suis pas moins homme.

In the end, she is impelled by her passion to declare love for Clitandre, even to the point of asking him to marry her, the ultimate indignity for this campaigner for female equality. But she cannot bring herself to be honest, to openly admit that she loves and wants Clitandre; she can only do it through euphemisms and further hypocrisy. The scene is Act 4, Scene II. Armande pretends that she is reluctant to suggest such a course of action, since she is really above such base desires, but she doesn't quite succeed in concealing her own yearning. She dare not actually pronounce the word 'marriage', but has to descend to a pathetic circumlocution: 'ce dont il s'agit'.

Armande claims to have nothing but contempt for pleasures of the flesh, but she is a woman whose every night is tormented with erotic dreams.

3. Chrysale

The pathetic little husband in this household dominated by

women spends a lot of time persuading himself, in private, that he is master in his own home. Then, as soon as his wife appears on the scene, his plans to reassert his authority all vanish in a trice. He is 'd'une humeur à consentir à tout'. He is a little like Justice Shallow when he speaks with loving nostalgia of the days when he and his brother Ariste were young. Now, Ariste reminds him that his wife has him in the palm of her hand:

> Et votre lâcheté mérite qu'on en rie.

For all his suffering, we can have little sympathy for Chrysale. He reveals himself to be very concerned about the figure he cuts with the world, and his ideas that 'a woman's place is in the home' are too narrow-minded to be taken seriously; they were certainly not intended by Molière to represent his own views, as some critics, seduced by the diametric opposition between this and Philaminte's views, have claimed. In this matter, Chrysale is no better than Arnolphe in *L'École des Femmes*.

4. Henriette

Almost every critic who has written about *Les Femmes Savantes* has found Henriette to be Molière's ideal maiden. The one exception is Antoine Adam, who calls her hateful. In her favour, she is reasonable, charming, intelligent and subtle. She also speaks her mind. However, while not wishing to agree with Adam's harsh judgement, we find it difficult to believe that Molière's ideal would proclaim anything as unambitious and silly as:

> Je me trouve fort bien, ma mère, d'être bête.

If one must look for Molière's ideal woman, one is far more likely to find her in *L'Avare*.

Like all the young heroines, Henriette has some pertinent things to say about marriage, of which we shall quote only two lines:

> Mais savez-vous qu'on risque un peu plus qu'on ne pense
> A vouloir sur un coeur user de violence.

5. Clitandre

C'est un bavard qui a toujours à la bouche le mot de sincérité. Il n'est jamais las d'affirmer que ses intentions sont pures. Il étale les preuves de sa vertu, il se frappe la poitrine.   (Antoine Adam)

This may be. But one would be hard put to it to deny the justice and good sense of much of what Clitandre says on the subjects of pedantry and ambitious women, and in these scenes at least, he must surely be Molière's spokesman.

Un sot savant est plus sot qu'un sot ignorant.

Or, a little knowledge is a dangerous thing.

Clitandre recalls the principles of Alceste (in *Le Misanthrope*) when he refuses to praise the works of Trissotin, which he finds worthless (Act 1, Scene III), and his praise for the Court (Act 4, Scene III) is most definitely in agreement with Molière's own feelings.

6. Trissotin

Trissotin is one of the nastiest characters Molière created. Bursting with an overwhelming vanity and narcissistic self-esteem, he accounts himself not only a good poet but a famous one, and assumes that his celebrity gives him the unalienable right to look with contempt upon everyone else. In reality, his poems are appalling. He is one of those authors who are:

De leurs vers fatigants lecteurs infatigables.

All this would be harmless enough, were it not for the hidden side of his character, which is not revealed until Act 5, Scene I, when we discover a cynical, unscrupulous machiavellian:

Pourvu que je vous aie, il n'importe comment,

he says to Henriette. She then finds before her a lecherous villain, itching with desire to get his hands on her. At this point, he is no longer an amusing character, but a despicable one.

Molière's contemporaries thought that the character of

Trissotin was a savage caricature of a well-known 'bad poet' of the time – l'abbé Cotin. According to R. Jasinski, Molière's first name for the character was Tricotin, and the sonnets he uses were lifted textually from Cotin's works. The other poet, Vadius, was similarly an unkind portrait of Ménage.

7. Bélise

Bélise is a middle-aged woman nurtured on novels of gallant love and conquest, with the result that she now lives on a cloud, quite divorced from the reality of everyday life, and is happy in her illusion that all the best-looking young men of Paris are fighting with each other to win her heart. Her language recalls the elaborate, flowery phrases of Madeleine de Scudéry's interminable novels. She carries an exact copy of La Carte du Tendre, the mainstay of the Précieuses, in her head (see Chapter 2), and consults it at every opportunity to discover what should be her next move in the Game of Love. Her scene with Clitandre is hilarious, since she interprets everything he says to her as a gallant stratagem with which to gain her affections. Although a little pedantic and snobbish, Bélise is far too amusing for the audience ever to fall out of sympathy with her as they do with Trissotin. This delightful old spinster is one of Molière's happiest creations, a serenely ridiculous study in self-delusion.

8. Martine

    (a) La poule ne doit pas chanter devant le coq.
    (b) Il lui faut un mari, non pas un pédagogue.
    (c) Les livres cadrent mal avec le mariage.
    (d) Quand on se fait entendre, on parle toujours bien.

Simple, honest, peasant, feminine good sense. A pleasing antidote to the pontifications of Philaminte and Armande.

9. The Intentions of the Author

At first sight, Les Femmes Savantes seems to contradict all the conclusions of L'École des Femmes. For ten years past, Molière had been clearly in favour of the emancipation of women, and had championed freedom for the fair sex in all its aspects – intellectual, marital, social. By showing the results of such freedom in the persons of Philaminte, Armande and Bélise, he now seems to deny his own precepts. This is in fact only a superficial appearance.

Molière wishes to satirize and condemn, not the quest for knowledge in itself, but the manic desire to know *everything*, and for the wrong reasons. He considers knowledge and learning to be worthless when the motive for acquiring them is vanity or self-glorification (cf. M. Jourdain in *Le Bourgeois Gentilhomme*). This sort of conceited pedantry leads not to learning, but to a blind acceptance of the written word, and of literary formulas and dogmas. Voltaire put it very neatly:

> Molière n'a pas assurément prétendu, en attaquant les femmes savantes, se moquer de la science et de l'esprit. Il n'en a joué que l'abus et l'affectation.

Indeed, we need not go as far as Voltaire for conviction on the matter. If we are still in any doubt as to Molière's intentions, we can refer to his Preface to *Les Précieuses Ridicules* (1959), which is relevant:

> les plus excellentes choses sont sujettes à être copiées par de mauvais singes, qui méritent d'être bernés; ces vicieuses imitations de ce qu'il y a de plus parfait ont été de tout temps la matière de la comédie.

or to the words of Clitandre in the very play which we are considering:

> Je consens qu'une femme ait des clartés de tout,
> Mais je ne lui veux point la passion choquante
> De se rendre savante afin d'être savante.

> Et qu'elle ait du savoir sans vouloir qu'on le sache,
> Sans citer des auteurs, sans dire de grands mots,
> Et clouer de l'esprit à ses moindres propos.

Je hais seulement
La science et l'esprit qui gâtent les personnes.

and, speaking of the authors whom such women follow:

Inhabiles à tout, vides de sens commun,
Et pleins d'un ridicule et d'une impertinence
A décrier partout l'esprit et la science.

11

Le Malade Imaginaire

Le Malade Imaginaire was presented on 10 February 1673. It was to be Molière's last play, for he died a few hours after the fourth performance on 17 February.

1. Argan

The Hypochondriac at the centre of the play belongs to the gallery of credulous fools from whom Molière drew some of his most comic creations (Harpagon in *L'Avare*, Monsieur Jourdain in *Le Bourgeois Gentilhomme*, etc.). He is not only easily taken in by the opportunist doctors, but by his wife as well. He is obsessed with the idea of illness, and is convinced that he is particularly vulnerable to every germ under the sun. He is also nervous, irritable, and selfish, but these traits stem directly from his obsession, or are aggravated by it. He tries to appear terrifying and authoritarian, but does not succeed in hiding his native sensitivity before his little daughter Louison. He does not have the courage to speak up against the doctors, not even against his impudent servant Toinette, who openly treats him as a child:

> Ces messieurs-là s'égayent bien sur votre corps; ils ont en vous une bonne vache à lait.

The psychological accuracy of the portrait is remarkable. Argan's only satisfaction in life is to brood upon his disabilities. By convincing himself that he is ill, he does in fact become mentally deranged.

Molière himself played this part and was unwell during all four performances. The tragic irony of the situation is all too apparent. Jasinski refers to 'un extraordinaire humour noir'. The author was seized with some sort of attack during the fourth performance, which was noticed by the audience, but he continued until the end. He complained of feeling cold, and was taken to his home near by, where he later started to spit blood. His wife Armande called two priests, who refused to come to the dying man and administer last rites. A third priest who did agree to get out of bed for Molière arrived too late.

2. Béline

Antoine Adam calls her 'doucereuse et sinistre'. She is the wife who takes advantage of her husband's naïvety to win his confidence and pocket his money after his death. She calls him her 'pauvre petit mari' or her 'petit fils', but her real attitude towards Argan is not revealed until the scene in which she believes him dead. Her terrible greed and hardness recall the more modern characters later to be created by François Mauriac.

3. Angélique

> Angélique, c'est la naissance de l'amour, ses divines naïvetés, sa surprise émerveillée. Elle défend âprement son bonheur et mêle la candeur à la rouerie.
>
> (Antoine Adam)

She holds her own very well indeed against her mother, and is clearsighted enough to see through her sugary protests of affection. Angélique's firm and slightly hostile attitude towards her mother contrasts with her sincere affection and respect for her father. Thinking he is dead, she shows a spontaneous grief so intense as to lead her to renounce her lover out of respect for his memory, since he had wanted her to marry the doctor's idiot son.

Like most of Molière's young heroines, she is given ample opportunity to defend the rights of young ladies to choose their own husbands:

Le mariage est une chaine où l'on ne doit jamais soumettre un coeur par force.

4. Toinette

Elle a de la verve et de l'impertinence, elle est fine et bonne, gaillarde et joyeuse. Elle est pleine de tendresse pour les jeunes gens et pour les amoureux.

(Antoine Adam)

She is given much more character than most of Molière's servants, who are usually content merely to be on the right side and to be impertinent and obstructive. Toinette, on the other hand, is a fully-rounded character with a sparkling wit all her own:

(a) Est-ce que nous ne pouvons pas raisonner ensemble sans nous emporter?

(b) Ne parlez pas si haut, de peur d'ébranler le cerveau de monsieur.

(c) Quand un maître ne songe pas à ce qu'il fait, une servante bien sensée est en droit de le redresser.

5. Thomas Diafoirius

This man is a caricature of the academic faction, very influential in the France of 1673, which was traditionalist in its approach to medicine (and indeed to all branches of science), and held that modern scientific progress was bad *per se* since it was not founded on the irrefutable teachings of Aristotle. Such blind reactionaries are always to be found in opposition whenever modern experimentation achieves any success, but they were particularly powerful in the medical profession at this time. (This is not to say that the entire medical profession was crass, only that it counted many reactionaries in its ranks.)

Diafoirius is one of Molière's most gloriously stupid creations. He is a curious mixture of the pedant and the village idiot. He speaks like a book; in fact, his 'knowledge' is clearly learnt by heart from Aristotle and can only be mouthed by him, puppet-fashion. He greets Angélique as his future mother-in-law (a grotesquely gauche mistake if ever there was one), and forgets his carefully-rehearsed speech to her when Béline interrupts him and makes him lose the thread. Like a mere infant, he turns to his father for assistance or advice at the slightest excuse.

(a) Il s'attache aveuglément aux opinions de nos anciens, et jamais il n'a voulu comprendre ni écouter les raisons et les expériences des prétendues découvertes de notre siècle touchant la circulation du sang et autres opinions de la même farine.

(b) Avec une robe et un bonnet, tout galimatias devient savant, et toute sottise devient raison.   (Béralde)

6. The Play

Both Adam and Sarcey agree that *Le Malade Imaginaire* is a masterpiece of gaity, strength, and construction. Molière's sympathy for young lovers is shown more strongly here than in any other play. Although the play is technically a 'comédie-ballet' with three interludes of song and dance (between the acts and at the end), Molière puts an almost personal note in the songs of the second interlude, where the reader cannot resist the temptation, perhaps a little too imaginative, to assume that the author knew he was about to die and so allowed this final lyrical expression of his faith in youth, coloured with terrible melancholy, to remain as a personal epitaph:

Profitez du printemps
De vos beaux ans,
Aimable jeunesse.
Ne perdez point ces précieux moments;
La beauté passe,
Le temps s'efface,
L'âge de glace
Vient à sa place.

Another indication that Molière wanted to get the record straight and set his thoughts out clearly in this final play after eleven years of struggle with merciless adversaries who sought to distort or dilute that thought, is the extraordinary Scene III of Act 3, when Argan and Béralde calmly and intelligently discuss the plays of Molière; the scene is quite out of tone with the rest of the play; there is no action, and nothing amusing. The play stops for a while to permit Molière, through Béralde (and who could deny that this otherwise unnecessary character is Molière's deliberate mouthpiece?), to set forth in clear explanatory terms, his attitude towards the medical profession, towards the age in which he lives, towards the purpose of comedy in the theatre, towards his own position vis-à-vis his work. It is a very important scene, which could be read in isolation; he insists that his satire is meant to point the finger of rebuke only at those who *abuse* certain cherished principles, and not at the principles themselves, which he had previously said at the very beginning of his career in Paris, in the Preface to *Les Précieuses Ridicules*, and, more recently, in Clitandre's speech in *Les Femmes Savantes*. We are already familiar with the 'plot' of the play, which had already been used by Molière in other works – a household thrown into disarray by the selfish obsession of the head of the house, who threatens to destroy his daughter's happiness by marrying her to someone whom she does not love.

7. The Intentions of Molière

1. Molière, en écrivant *Le Malade Imaginaire,* veut faire la satire de la Faculté de Médecine. Il n'est pas un simple amuseur. Il prétend railler certaines erreurs, affirmer une attitude, une doctrine. Contre la médecine, il ose dire son hostilité.   (Antoine Adam)

Here is Molière's scepticism in his own words, through the character of Béralde:

les ressorts de notre machine sont des mystères, jusques ici, où les hommes ne voient goutte, et la nature nous a mis au-devant des yeux des voiles trop épais pour y connaître quelque chose.

2. Some doctors know full well how limited their abilities are, but find it more profitable not to disclose their ignorance. Others are genuinely naïve, and these are possibly more dangerous:

   C'est de la meilleure foi du monde qu'il vous expédiera.
                                                    (Béralde)

3. It has been suggested that the play represents Molière's answer to a particularly vitriolic pamphlet which had been written against him some years before, *Élomire Hypocondre*. Élomire is clearly an anagram of Molière. This would suppose that Molière confirms the attacks of his enemies, and admits that he is, as they say, a hypochondriac, mentally sick and obsessed. To say the least, this is highly unlikely. It is however possible that the subject at least of the play was suggested by *Élomire Hypocondre*.

12

Conclusions

A. Purpose

The student who attempts to dig deep into an author's mind, to interpret where interpretation is unnecessary, to seek to establish a continuous thread of purpose and meaning throughout his work, runs the risk of discovering a message which isn't there, or at best uncovering the wrong message. The pages of literary criticism are strewn with mistaken conceptions of Molière's 'real' philosophy, born for the most part from an obsessive preoccupation with categories and labels. French criticism, in particular, is plagued with this spirit of organization and analysis, especially in the nineteenth century. Molière defies such trite classification. His attitude towards the nobility, for example, cannot be said to be the same in *Le Misanthrope* as it is in *Le Bourgeois Gentilhomme*, nor are his views on the rights of women entirely commensurate with his derision of those women who attain these rights. It is therefore dangerous to read between the lines, as it were, and the safest way to arrive at a correct idea of Molière's purpose is to rely completely and solely on what Molière himself said was his purpose. He spelt it out quite clearly in a number of his prefaces, and in *La Critique de L'École des Femmes*.

Molière's avowed aim is two-fold:

(*a*) de corriger les hommes en les divertissant
(*b*) d'attaquer, par des peintures ridicules, les vices de ce siècle.

These purposes are clearly two sides of the same coin. At the beginning of his career in Paris, Molière wrote, in his Preface to *Les Précieuses Ridicules*, the following lines:

> Les plus excellentes choses sont sujettes à être copiées par de mauvais singes, qui méritent d'être bernés; ces vicieuses imitations de ce qu'il y a de plus parfait ont été de tout temps la matière de la comédie.

He goes on to say that the true Précieuses should not feel outraged if those empty-headed fools who copy them are pilloried on stage for doing the job badly. Four years later, in *La Critique de L'École de Femmes*, Molière repeats the point:

> (the aims of Comedy are) de rendre agréablement sur le théâtre les défauts de tout le monde. Vous n'avez rien fait, si vous n'y faites reconnaître les gens de votre siècle.

In other words, to achieve his declared purpose of improving the society in which he lives, by ridiculing its worst aspects, it is important that Molière's portraits should be instantly recognizable by the audience as representing certain contemporary types; truth is therefore of the essence in these caricatures.

Furthermore, truth is impartial, and knows no exceptions. If Monsieur Jourdain (in *Le Bourgeois Gentilhomme*) can be ridiculed for his social-climbing antics, so can Orgon (in *Tartuffe*) for allowing his values to be warped by a religious fanatic; the social pretensions of those who wished to 'keep up with the Joneses', and the religious pretensions of hypocritical puritans, were equally dangerous and equally ridiculous. In his Preface to *Tartuffe*, Molière writes:

> Si l'emploi de la comédie est de corriger les vices des hommes, je ne vois pas par quelle raison il y en aura de privilégiés.

The student might also read the Premier Placet, where this idea is repeated with greater emphasis.

Should there be any doubt left as to the candid simplicity of Molière's purpose in writing, we may turn to the comment of

Donneau de Visé who, as a contemporary and friend of Molière, is in a better position to know the intentions of his colleague than the subsequent critics. In his *Lettre sur le Misanthrope*, Donneau said that Molière

> n'a point voulu faire une comédie pleine d'incidents, mais une pièce, seulement, où il pût parler contre les moeurs du siècle.

To summarize, Molière was a man of the theatre, an entertainer, but he was also a teacher. The provocation of laughter was rarely (though sometimes) a simple end in itself. He wanted his work to be useful and instructive.

B. Principal Ideas

1. Faith in Human Nature

In spite of the contempt which he shows for many social types which surround him, Molière has a deep faith in human nature. He is wholeheartedly in sympathy with youth which is bursting with energy and desire to live, and quite unsullied with the envy, ambition and cynicism of the older generation. He is likewise an adorer of love which is innocent, spontaneous, reciprocated and healthy. Though one may not think so at first glance, Molière also has faith in human society. It is better than any possible 'school' as a means towards real education. He speaks often of 'l'école du monde', and believes that social life is the best power for education, and, in so far as it is opposed to pedantry, it is also a liberating force.

2. Les mauvais singes

This heading is lifted from the Preface to *Les Précieuses Ridicules*, quoted above. The subjects of all Molière's attacks have one thing in common, they are all 'mauvais singes', counterfeiters, imitators. Religious hypocrites who don't believe in God, doctors who don't believe in medicine, literary critics who don't understand literature, prudes who are secretly consumed with desire, snobs who pretend to be what they are not, and so on. They are all counterfeiters, whose words lack sincerity. This Molière despises above all else, and he sees the society in which he lives threatened with mediocrity as a result of the influence of false values and blind adulation for the second-rate. If there is a moral lesson in Molière's writings, it is not so much to be found in the maxims volunteered by his 'raisonneurs', but in his long, personal fight against lies and liars. 'Tous les hommes sont semblables par les paroles, et ce n'est que les actions qui les découvrent différents' says Élise in *L'Avare*. Molière showed with signal success how empty were the words of liars, and how their deeds betrayed them. Tartuffe's avowed chastity is shattered when he is alone with Elmire and cannot resist putting a furtive hand on her knee. Trissotin (in *Les Femmes Savantes*) and Oronte (in *Le Misanthrope*) appear to be poets until they recite their absurd verses with all the attendant mannerisms which we nowadays call 'camp'. We are inclined to believe Armande's (in *Les Femmes Savantes*) self-righteousness until we see her trembling with desire for Clitandre. All try to pull the wool over our eyes (and sometimes over their own eyes as well), and in the end none succeed, for truth will out, and sincerity wins through in the long run.

3. Modernist

If Molière lived now, one might be tempted to call him an 'écrivain engagé', or even a muted Socialist. His works campaign for the emancipation of women (to a limited extent), for the spread of liberal education (again, within reason), for a check to the stultifying power of the Church, and for a break with blind obedience to established doctrines. This last example of a 'modernist' attitude towards cultural evolution is especially apparent in *Le Malade Imaginaire*. Those who unquestioningly obey the Aristotelian rules concerning medicine are mocked; those who, like Béralde, express confidence in the modern theories of the circulation of the blood, and so on, speak with authority. Similarly, Molière's attitude towards the classical rules of the theatre, which also owed their origin to Aristotle, is irreverent. In *La Critique de l'École des Femmes*, he points out that a play which entertains the audience is good, whether or not it obeys the rules, and that if a perfectly 'regular' play is a bore, then it follows that the rules are not very good. In many ways, therefore, Molière is an innovator and a modernist.

C. Principles

Although Molière wishes to 'corriger les hommes', he does not have a doctrine or a precise moral lesson to teach his audiences. His plays reveal an antipathy towards any form of dogmatism, so he is unlikely to be dogmatic himself. Loret is very much mistaken when he claims that, reading the plays of Molière, 'on entend un prédicateur.'

Of course, Molière does have moral and ethical principles, but they are certainly not to be discovered in the self-righteous moralizing of his 'raisonneurs', such as Ariste in *L'École des Maris*, Chrysalde in *L'École des Femmes*; these are more representative of the prudent pragmatism of the bourgeois, and their principles are at best superficial or negative. Molière's own ethical ideas, which permeate all his work and are just as easily gleaned, are more positive.

His first principle is a trust in the fundamental goodness of human nature, when it is innocent and unspoilt or unsullied by envy, ambition, or prejudice. A number of characters would serve to illustrate this point. Elmire in *Tartuffe* compromises her virtue and allows herself to be submitted to sordid seduction only in order to save her family and reveal the truth to her besotted husband. Agnès in *L'École des Femmes*, though ignorant of the ways of the world, retains that lucidity and common sense with which her natural intelligence endows her.

The converse of this ethic is of course a hatred of moral pedantry and asceticism. The saintly hypocrisy of a Tartuffe or the wily maxims of an Arnolphe (in *L'École des Femmes*) are anathema to a lover of simplicity and honesty such as Molière.

We must return for a moment to consider the importance or otherwise of the raisonneurs, if only because they have assumed in many a respected critical work a significance which they do not deserve. Does Molière advocate the 'middle way'? Attempts have been made to prove that Molière's morality consisted in finding the 'juste milieu' between possible extremes, such as is sought by Ariste (in *L'École des Maris*), Chrysalde (in *L'École des Femmes*), and especially Philinte in *Le Misanthrope*, who is the most articulate and persuasive supporter of this view, if only because Alceste is so extreme in his attachment to honesty. But these characters, if one reads their words carefully, express mediocre, thoughtless, and essentially bourgeois principles. They boil down to a cautious conformity to all established patterns of behaviour, for fear of shocking public opinion. The raisonneurs want above all not to 'épater le bourgeois', to avoid fuss, and to get on in life quietly and comfortably. They are the apostles of compromise, and their opinions would be unworthy of Molière. R. Jasinski, in his recent book, is the latest critic to support this view, although he does modify it somewhat, and with conviction. 'Entre les excès il cherche un juste milieu,' he writes, 'non banal et conformiste, mais éclairé, nuancé, ennemi des vaines chimères et pourtant généreux.' (op. cit. p. 272.)

It has also been suggested by some literary commentators that Molière is epicurean, that he exalts the joys of Instinct. Jules Lemaitre is certainly correct to write that he is an enemy of austerity, that he detests arbitrary restrictions on people, that he hates pretence, that he is the very opposite of Pascal or Polyeucte (in Corneille's play *Polyeucte*). But the Catholic writer Brunetière carries the idea too far when he says that Molière is an Apostle of Nature, in the manner of Jean-Jacques Rousseau, and that he recommended the free, unbridled expression of all natural instincts.

Certainly, one of Molière's most cherished principles is a faith in human nature, as we have noted above, but it is a human nature which seeks to rise above the level of mere animal satisfactions. All the heroines who represent this ideal, such as Agnès in *L'École des Femmes*, Henriette in *Les Femmes Savantes*, or Élise in *L'Avare*, are for the most part intelligent and perspicacious; they are not merely instinctive hedonists.

There is a further objection to Brunetière's argument. For the Rousseauesque Apostle of Nature, nothing is more artificial and thereby detestable than organized Society. And yet we have seen that Molière respects the value of social life as a force for education and good. Moreover, his most ridiculous characters are anti-social. They are ridiculous because they wish to escape Society entirely and live in their own selfish little world, made of egoism or envy. Arnolphe (in *L'École des Femmes*) is the epitome of selfishness, Dom Juan the arch-egotist. Even Monsieur Jourdain (in *Le Bourgeois Gentilhomme*), the social climber is less interested in the value of social life than in the figure which he himself can cut in Society.

D. Molière's Religion

In 1663, Molière was very friendly with the iconoclastic freethinkers of La Croix Blanche, and in particular La Mothe le Vayer. He also knew Boileau later. It is possible that these writers and their ideas had some influence on his religious views, and it is perhaps significant that he wrote *Tartuffe* in the winter of 1663–4. He did not leave us any precise indication of his personal religious beliefs, but it is quite clear that he did not subscribe to the rigorous idea that there is no salvation outside the Church. Religious orthodoxy is foreign to his conception of the good life, because it is blind, destructive, anti-human. Molière's own attitude must be much closer to a tolerant humanism. Then one must not omit a consideration of the shocking character of Dom Juan. He is a machiavellian, demonstrably without religious beliefs of any kind. The play is unquestionably blasphemous. All the traditional proofs of the existence of God are ridiculed by him, and the concept of after-life he likewise mercilessly derides. Sganarelle's arguments in favour of Christian faith are too absurd to gain any credence, Molière gives the task of defending God to a mere servant who cannot open his mouth without saying something stupid, and Molière himself played this part. By contrast, the blasphemous Don Juan is both articulate and persuasive. He is also, however, supremely selfish, a sensual hedonist who has no respect for anything, and does not gain ours. It would be rash, therefore, to conclude that Molière was himself as anti-Christian as Don Juan.

Equally condemnable are the 'automatic' Christians, such as Orgon and Mme Pernelle in *Tartuffe*, or Arnolphe in *L'École des Femmes*. Their faith consists only in obedience to established codes and precepts, which they have learnt and never question. Molière leaves us in no doubt that he views such lip-service with contempt. Actions are more important and revelatory than the perfect recital of a catechism.

On the other hand, although he denounced 'les faux dévots' in *Tartuffe*, he took pains to contrast them with 'les dévots de coeur', who, he wrote, 'par leurs actions reprennent les nôtres, et leur dévotion est humaine et traitable.' While campaigning both against the rigours of asceticism and intolerance on the one hand, and against the moral turpitude of hypocrisy on the other, he seems to maintain that one can love God through a love of human kind, and that one can achieve salvation while still living a full and happy life.

E. Education of Girls

Arnolphe in *L'École des Femmes*, Sganarelle in *L'École des Maris*, and Chrysale in *Les Femmes Savantes* all insist that girls should remain in complete and utter ignorance, while the first two are in addition partisans of the most rigid denial of personal liberty. Molière's own convictions are completely contrary to these. He believes that virtue, to have any value at all, must be freely embraced, and cannot be enforced by discipline:

C'est l'honneur qui les doit tenir dans le devoir,
Non la sévérité que nous leur faisons voir.
(*L'École des Maris*)

F. Marriage

The theme of marriage and filial liberty serves Molière in two ways:

1. As the basic plot in almost all his plays.
2. As an illustration of his sympathy for youth.

Although Molière's views on marriage are consistent throughout his work, from Gorgibus in *Les Précieuses Ridicules*, to Angélique in *Le Malade Imaginaire*, it would be wrong to suppose that they represented any profound, revolutionary, or original thought. They are identical with views already current in Précieux circles in 1640–50. But they are important, in so far as they show more clearly than anything else Molière's sensitivity and kindness, the value he places upon honesty in human relations, and on love, freely entered into on both sides, and reciprocal.

'Le mariage est une chose sainte et sacrée', says Gorgibus in *Les Précieuses Ridicules*. It is an equal partnership between two willing persons, founded upon love and mutual respect rather than obedience and possession. Valère in *L'Avare* says that 'le mariage est une plus grande affaire qu'on ne peut croire; qu'il y va d'être heureux ou malheureux toute sa vie, et qu'un engagement qui doit durer jusqu'à la mort ne se doit jamais faire qu'avec de grandes précautions.' Above all, a marriage must not be arranged by parents in spite of the wishes of their children, nor must it rest on the obedience and subservience of the wife to the husband, as Arnolphe would have Agnès so dependent (in *L'École des Femmes*). The best definition of marriage is found in *Le Misanthrope*. Alceste refuses Célimène,

Pusique vous n'êtes pas, en des liens si doux
Pour trouver tout en moi comme moi tout en vous.

In other words, a successful marriage can only exist where each partner lives to make the other happy and content. This is as wise and as true now as it was in Molière's day. It is perhaps his most constructive message, and the one which renders his plays so heart-warming.

G. La Préciosité

This subject has already been dealt with in some detail in Chapter 2, but a few words of clarification are worth while here.

1. (a) There are a few instances (for example in *L'Avare*) where Molière's language is distinctly *précieux* in style.

(b) Molière supports wholeheartedly one idea in the précieux canon, and that is the concept that real virtue is an inner quality, not a system of rules imposed from without; that one must freely adopt a virtuous way of life, aware of all the alternatives, and not just offer obedience to a strict moral code. As Ariste points out in *L'École des Maris*, true chastity of mind does not need to be enforced, and when it is, it is worthless.

2. (a) But Molière satirized the over-abundance of sentiment to which the highly-developed Précieux sensibility had given rise, and as a result of which a Précieuse could not love without fear and trembling, could not be loved without dying with ecstasy, could not be refused without wasting away with despair.

(b) He also dislikes affectation in language and manners, insincerity of opinion, the thirst for knowledge only to be seen to be knowledgeable, all of which are aspects of the egoism peculiarly exaggerated and nurtured by Preciosity.

(c) He further despises the aberration of prudery, which was a lamentable by-product of the Précieux attitude towards love. Cathos in *Les Précieuses Ridicules*, is the first in the gallery of prudes, but she is merely funny, whereas the later

Arsinoé in *Le Misanthrope* and Armande in *Les Femmes Savantes* are respectively pitiful and hateful. Arsinoé, 'qui tâche à couvrir d'un faux voile de prude Ce que chez elle on voit d'affreuse solitude,' in the bitter words of Célimène, is a wasted, lonely, middle-aged woman, whose spontaneity and ability to react genuinely and honestly towards people have been stifled and corrupted by an unhealthy attitude towards love. Pursuing a loved one was, for the Précieux, rather like a game of chess, but more laborious. Madeleine de Scudéry had indeed published a map to guide the uninitiated. Arsinoé, who had been Précieuse in her youth, can remember only the rules, which she tries unsuccessfully on Alceste, and has forgotten the heart. She plays the game correctly, pretends to be hard to get, and cannot understand why it doesn't work, and she is left an old maid. She is pathetic. Armande is more of a hypocrite. Her erotic designs on Clitandre are all too clear, yet she talks of sexual love with contempt and loathing. One imagines this frustrated spinster admiring her naked body in her bedroom mirror; yet she is not to be pitied. Her frustration is the deserved result of base hypocrisy.

The servant Dorine in *Tartuffe* perfectly summarizes Molière's derisory view of the prude:

Hautement d'un chacun elles blâment la vie
Non point par charité, mais par un trait d'envie
Qui ne saurait souffrir qu'une autre ait les plaisirs
Dont le penchant de l'âge a sevré leurs désirs.

Riddled with envy and self-pity, the prude is the very antithesis of the joyful, gladdening, and wise innocence of an Agnès.

H. The Marquesses

Molière made frequent and merciless fun of the young marquesses who were a feature of court life, and showed them for the most part inanely silly and infatuated with their own importance. Impostors who had taken the title of marquess without any real right to it were abundant in mid-seventeenth-century France.

The first marquess is Mascarille in *Les Précieuses Ridicules*. But the most amusing and cleverly drawn are Acaste and Clitandre in *Le Misanthrope*. Preening themselves before each other, vying for attention, laden with jewels, fine clothes and absurdly ornate wigs, they, like almost every character whom Molière mocks, are prisoners of their own egoism. They are blinkered by their gorgeous curls, and consider the rest of the world is there to admire them.

But Molière went to pains to point out that he was not satirizing marquesses as such, but only those whose extravagances made them a laughing-stock, and whose sycophancy made them detestable, 'ces obligeants diseurs d'inutiles paroles'. Is it necessary to remind the reader of the many prefaces in which Molière insisted that genuine persons need not feel annoyed if clowns who imitate them badly are lampooned?

I. The Doctors

Molière satirizes the medical profession for its pedantry, its blind loyalty to traditional cures, its ritual, its respect for an outdated orthodoxy. He seems to suggest, in both *Dom Juan* and *Le Malade Imaginaire*, that Nature and Luck have more credit for medical cures than do the doctors. Again, the worst doctors are those, like Diafoirius (in *Le Malade Imaginaire*), whose *egoism* and pride in their useless knowledge make them incapable of learning from the world outside their ancient moth-eaten books.

J. Complexity of Character

1. Molière does initially base his characters upon social types, which recur throughout his work. The most common of these is Sganarelle/Arnolphe/Orgon (in *L'École des Maris*, *L'École des Femmes*, and *Tartuffe*), the little man with petty ideas and even pettier obsessions, unaware of his own insig-

nificance because he is blind to the world around him, and insisting stubbornly that he is right and everybody else is wrong.

2. Nevertheless, on this basis of social types, Molière created real characters who sprung to life, and who were drawn more from life than from dramatic theory. Since they are drawn from life, they may not be completely predictable. Dorante in *La Critique de L'École des Femmes*, says that 'il n'est pas incompatible qu'une personne soit ridicule en de certaines choses et honnête homme en d'autres.' This may be applied to Alceste (in *Le Misanthrope*), and even to M. Jourdain (in *Le Bourgeois Gentilhomme*).

Donneau de Visé, in his *Lettre sur Le Misanthrope*, defended the truthfulness of Molière's portraits against charges that they were illogical.

K. Personal Satire

Not only were Molière's characters drawn from life, they were often drawn from living contemporaries. Although, for reasons of obvious prudence, Molière always claimed that his characters were entirely fictitious, and that his satire only fell upon certain individuals obliquely and by accident (see Uranie's speech in *La Critique de L'École des Femmes*), we may be allowed to suppose that at least some of the identifications which have been suggested have at least a grain of truth in them. Vicious literary polemics were, after all, a daily amusement in Molière's day.

Trissotin in *Les Femmes Savantes* is said to be based on the well-known Précieux poet l'Abbé Cotin, and Vadius on Ménage. *Tartuffe* is a barely disguised spoof on l'Abbé Roquette, who was known to behave in like manner, and *l'Amour Médecin* is based on five known doctors. There can only be conjecture about Alceste (in *Le Misanthrope*), who is traditionally supposed to be a portrait of Molière himself, and about Monsieur Jourdain (in *Le Bourgeois Gentilhomme*), who could conceivably be an unkind caricature of Colbert.

It should be remembered that the climate at Versailles under Louis XIV was particularly liberal, and it was permitted to poke fun at anyone, provided the King and the Royal Household were respected. It was also a matter of course that the intention to satirize a known person should be vigorously denied. In his many battles against hypocrisy (following, for example, the performances of *L'École des Femmes* and *Tartuffe*), Molière was often accused of libellous portraits, and his greatest champion in such cases was often Louis XIV himself.

L. The Rules

Molière has little respect for the Aristotelian rules of the theatre. He constantly disregards unity of time and place, and especially (except in *Le Misanthrope*) has no concern for the Rule of Probability. La Bruyère makes a big point of this failing in his book *Les Caractères*. Molière himself dismissed the subject as unworthy of serious consideration in *La Critique de l'École des Femmes*, in which Dorante says:

> La grande règle de toutes les règles est de plaire . . . et si les pièces qui sont elon les règles ne plaisent pas, et que celles qui plaisent ne soient pas selon les règles, il faudrait de nécessité que les règles eussent été mal faites.

The most common charge brought against Molière's disregard for dramatic tradition is that he offends in particular against the Unity of Tone, in that his comedies can often appear tragic. Alfred de Musset's comment on this is famous:

> Quelle mâle gaîté, si triste et si profonde
> Que, lorsqu'on vient d'en rire, on devrait en pleurer.

Molière would be flattered, rather than upset, by this view of his work. His purpose, we have discovered, is to correct the follies of mankind. His talent demands that he do this by entertaining us with some hilarious portraits of men and women whose obsessions have been carried to risible extremes.[1] But if we are to learn from them, we must be made to think, to reflect, and to conclude that they sometimes teach us something about ourselves, or at least awaken in us compassion for the follies of others. It is a tribute to the eternal art of Molière that audiences are still doing this, and that the *gaîté* is still very *mâle*.

---

[1] R. Jasinski is of the opinion that Molière would have preferred to write tragedies, and that the failure of his one attempt, *Dom Garcie de Navarre*, was a cruel disappointment to him. (op. cit. p. 51)

Chronology

15 January 1622: Marie Cressé, wife of Jean-Poquelin, gives birth to a boy, Jean-Baptiste Poquelin (later known as Molière), in a house in the rue Saint-Honoré, Paris.

1631: Jean Poquelin is appointed supplier of tapestries to H.M. The King, a position which also carries the honorary title of valet de chambre.

1632: Marie Cressé dies, and Jean Poquelin remarries.

16 June 1643: The Illustre Théâtre Company is formed under the leadership of Madeleine Béjart, with Jean-Baptiste Poquelin as a minor member.

1644: Poquelin assumes the stage name of Molière, and becomes Director of the Company.

1645: The Illustre Théâtre Company is disbanded owing to heavy debts.

1646: Molière and the Béjart family join Dufresne's Company, and begin their fifteen-year tour of the South of France.

1652: The Company finds a patron in Prince Conty. Molière is now the Director and Principal Actor.

1657: Prince Conty withdraws his patronage.

24 October 1658: The Company's first performance in Paris, in the presence of the King, at the Palais du Louvre. They play *Nicomède* and *Le Docteur Amoureux*, a farce. Monsieur, frère du Roy, becomes their new patron.

2 November 1658: They find a semi-permanent home at the Petit Bourbon theatre, which they must share with an Italian company for the best part of a year.

18 November 1659: Les Précieuses Ridicules.

1660: Molière's Company moves to the Palais Royal.

28 May 1660: Sganarelle.

4 February 1661: Dom Garcie de Navarre.

24 June 1661: L'École des Maris.

17 August 1661: Les Fâcheux.

20 February 1662: Molière marries Armande Béjart.

26 December 1662: L'École des Femmes.

1 June 1663: La Critique de L'École des Femmes.

14 October 1663: L'Impromptu de Versailles.

29 January 1664: Le Mariage Forcé.

8 May 1664: La Princesse d'Élide.

12 May 1664: Le Tartuffe. (First 3 acts only; immediately banned.)

25 February 1665: Dom Juan.

14 August 1665: Molière's Company given title 'The King's Troup'.

15 September 1665: L'Amour Médecine.

4 June 1666: Le Misanthrope.

6 August 1666: Le Médecin Malgré Lui.

5 August 1667: one performance of Le Tartuffe, in 5 acts; banned again.

13 January 1668: Amphitryon.

July 1668: Georges Dandin.

9 September 1668: L'Avare.

9 February 1669: Le Tartuffe.

25 February 1669: death of Molière's father.

4 February 1670: Les Amants Magnifiques.

14 October 1670: Le Bourgeois Gentilhomme.

17 January 1671: Psyché.

24 May 1671: Les Fourberies de Scapin.

2 December 1671: La Comtesse d'Escarbagnas.

14 February 1672: death of Madeleine Béjart.

11 March 1672: Les Femmes Savantes.

10 February 1673: Le Malade Imaginaire.

17 February 1673: death of Molière.

1677: foundation of Comédie Française.

Bibliography

Histoire de la Littérature Francaise au XVIIe Siècle by Antoine Adam. Volume 3 – L'Apogée du Siècle. Éditions Domat, Paris, 1952.

Histoire de la Poésie Française by Émile Faguet. Volume 13. Hatier-Boivin, Paris, 1927.

Questions de Critique by F. Brunetière. Calmann-Lévy, Paris, 1887.

La Préciosité et les Précieux by René Bray, Albin Michel, Paris, 1948.

Molière, a new criticism by W. G. Moore. Clarendon Press, Oxford, 1949.

Molière, l'homme et l'oeuvre by Daniel Mornet. Hatier-Boivin, Paris, 1943.

Jeunesse de Molière, Débuts de Molière à Paris, Les Luttes de Molière, three volumes by Gustave Michaud. Hachette, Paris, 1923–25.

Molière, homme de théâtre by René Bray. Mercure de France, Paris, 1954.

Molière par lui-même by Alfred Simon. Éditions du Seuil, Paris.

Molière et le Misanthrope by R. Jasinski. Colin, Paris, 1951.

Le Misanthrope de Molière by René Doumic. Éditions Mellottée, Paris.

Les Femmes Savantes de Molière by Gustave Reynier. Mellottée, Paris, 1937.

XVIIe Siècle by Lagarde et Michaud. Bordas, Paris.

Impressions de Théâtre by Jules Lemaître, 1888.

Molière by René Jasinski. Hatier, 1969.